WHISPERS OF THE GREEN: UNVEILING THE MYSTICAL LANGUAGE OF TREES

A Journey Through the Hidden Life of Forests

Holly Jane McConnell

S.D.N Publishing

Copyright © 2024 S.D.N Publishing

All rights reserved

The characters and events portrayed in this book are fictitious. Any similarity to real persons, living or dead, is coincidental and not intended by the author.

No part of this book may be reproduced, or stored in a retrieval system, or transmitted in any form or by any means, electronic, mechanical, photocopying, recording, or otherwise, without express written permission of the publisher.

ISBN: 9798876980748

CONTENTS

Title Page
Copyright
General Disclaimer   1
The Roots of Communication   3
The Silent Sentinels - Introduction to Tree Communication   4
Underground Networks - Exploring Mycorrhizal Fungi   8
The Language of Roots - Chemical Signaling Below Ground   12
The Life Above   15
The Whispering Leaves - Decoding Leaf Signals   16
The Breathing Bark - Tree Respiration and its Secrets   19
Floral Messages - Flowering and Communication   21
Seasonal Secrets   24
Spring Awakening - Tree Responses to Seasonal Change   25
Summer's Lush Conversations - Active Growth and Interaction   28
Autumnal Farewells - Preparing for Dormancy   32
The Forest Ecosystem   36
Inhabitants of the Canopy – Interactions with Birds and Insects   37
The Forest Floor - A World Below   40
Trees and the Cycle of Life - Death and Rebirth in the Forest   43

Historical Whispers	46
Ancient Trees - Witnesses of Time	47
Trees in Myth and Legend - Cultural Significance	49
Historic Trees - Stories They Tell	52
Trees and Humanity	55
Trees and Human Health - The Healing Power of Forests	56
The Trees That Feed Us - Fruit and Nut Trees	59
Sacred Groves - Spiritual and Religious Connections	62
Trees of the World	65
Rainforest Voices - The Lungs of the Earth	66
Ancient Bristlecones - The Oldest Living Trees	69
Trees of the Savannah - Adaptation and Survival	72
Trees and Climate	75
Trees and Carbon Sequestration - Fighting Climate Change	76
The Impact of Deforestation - A Global Issue	79
Reforestation - Hope for the Future	82
The Science of Trees	85
Understanding Tree Biology - From Seed to Giant	86
Tree Genetics - The Blueprint of Life	89
Modern Research - Uncovering New Secrets	92
Threats to Trees	98
Disease and Pests - Challenges Faced by Trees	99
Human Impact - Urbanization and its Effects	105
Conservation Efforts - Protecting Our Tree Heritage	111
Artistic Expressions	117
Trees in Art and Literature - Inspirational Muses	118
Photography and Trees - Capturing Their Essence	123
Trees in Film and Media - Symbolism and Representation	128

Toward the Future	133
Innovative Uses of Trees - Technology and Beyond	134
Trees in Urban Planning - Green Cities	139
The Legacy We Leave - Trees and Future Generations	143
Appendix A: Glossary of Terms	147
Appendix B: Resources for Further Reading	149
Appendix C: Links to Academic Papers and Journals	151
Appendix D: Tree Identification Guide	154
Appendix E: Conservation Organizations and Initiatives	167
Appendix F: Interactive Online Resources	171
THE END	175

GENERAL DISCLAIMER

This book is intended to provide general information to the reader on the topics covered. The author and publisher have made every effort to ensure that the information herein is accurate and up-to-date at the time of publication. However, they do not warrant or guarantee the accuracy, completeness, adequacy, or currency of the information contained in this book. The author and publisher expressly disclaim any liability or responsibility for any errors or omissions in the content herein.

The information, guidance, advice, tips, and suggestions provided in this book are not intended to replace professional advice or consultation. Readers are strongly encouraged to consult with an appropriate professional for specific advice tailored to their situation before making any decisions or taking any actions based on the content of this book.

The views and opinions expressed in this book are those of the author and do not necessarily reflect the official policy or position of any other agency, organization, employer or company.

The author and publisher are not responsible for any actions taken or not taken by the reader based on the information, advice, or suggestions provided in this book. The reader is solely responsible for their actions and the consequences thereof.

This book is not intended to be a source of legal, business, medical or psychological advice, and readers are cautioned to seek the services of a competent professional in these or other areas of expertise.

All product names, logos, and brands are property of their respective owners. All company, product and service names used in this book are for identification purposes only. Use of these names, logos, and brands does not imply endorsement.

Readers of this book are advised to do their own due diligence when it comes to making decisions and all information, products, services and advice that have been provided should be independently verified by your own qualified professionals.

By reading this book, you agree that the author and publisher are not responsible for your success or failure resulting from any information presented in this book.

THE ROOTS OF COMMUNICATION

THE SILENT SENTINELS - INTRODUCTION TO TREE COMMUNICATION

In the realm of forests, trees stand as silent sentinels, guardians of a hidden world teeming with life and interaction. Far from being mere static entities, trees engage in a sophisticated and intricate form of communication, essential for their survival and the wellbeing of the entire forest ecosystem.

The Language of Chlorophyll

Remarkably, trees communicate through various means, one of which involves the sharing of vital resources. An astonishing instance of this was observed in a beech tree stump, kept alive for centuries by surrounding trees through the transfer of sugars. This remarkable act of sustenance mirrors the behavior of elephant herds, showcasing a profound connection and care within the tree community.

Electrical and Chemical Signals

Trees also employ a complex system of chemical, hormonal, and slow-pulsing electrical signals. This communication bears a striking resemblance to animal nervous systems, although trees do not possess neurons or brains. These signals often convey messages of alarm or distress, forming a basic yet essential language for survival. For instance, researchers like Edward Farmer at the University of Lausanne have been delving into these electrical pulses, seeking to decode the hidden conversations of trees.

Scent Signals and Defensive Strategies

In the air, trees communicate using pheromones and other scent signals. A notable example is the umbrella thorn acacia in sub-Saharan Africa. When giraffes feed on its leaves, the tree emits ethylene gas as a distress signal, prompting neighboring acacias to produce tannins, deterring further grazing. This form of communication is so effective that giraffes have adapted to feed against the wind to avoid alerting other trees.

Furthermore, trees have a sense of taste and smell, allowing them to respond to specific threats. For example, when elms and pines are attacked by caterpillars, they can detect the saliva of the caterpillars and release pheromones to attract parasitic wasps, which then prey on the caterpillars, showcasing a sophisticated defensive mechanism.

Mycorrhizal Networks: The Wood Wide Web

Beneath the soil lies another dimension of tree communication: the mycorrhizal networks. These networks, likened to the nervous system of the forest, are crucial for tree health, especially in times of danger. Trees use this underground network to warn others about invasive predators or to inhibit the growth of invasive plant species. This system allows for a communal response to threats, enhancing the resilience of the forest as a whole.

Trees sharing a mycorrhizal network, like birch and fir, can send nutrients to each other or signal to each other in times of stress. This connection not only fortifies individual trees but also strengthens the forest ecosystem, making it more resilient to environmental stressors such as predators, toxins, and pathogenic microbes.

Climate Change and Forest Ecosystems

The health of these networks is directly impacted by climate change, which affects the biodiversity of the forest's microbiome. Changes in climate can disrupt the mycorrhizal networks, leading to altered tree morphology and a decrease in the photosynthetic capacity of trees. This, in turn, affects their growth and the carbon exchange with fungi. Thus, the resilience of trees to environmental changes is intimately linked to the health of their communication networks.

Mother Trees: Nurturers of the Forest

Central to these networks are the "mother trees," the largest and oldest trees in a forest, with extensive fungal connections. These trees play a nurturing role, distributing water and nutrients to neighboring trees and seedlings, especially when they detect distress signals. This supportive role of mother trees is crucial for the regeneration and overall health of the forest ecosystem.

Mother trees also facilitate a transfer of legacy from old to new generations. For instance, in response to injury or impending death, these trees can dump their carbon into the network for uptake by younger trees, ensuring continuity and resilience of the forest community.

The Future of Forest Stewardship

Understanding tree communication challenges our perception of trees as mere resources. It opens up a new dimension of forest stewardship, emphasizing the importance of preserving these complex communication networks. This knowledge can influence forestry practices, promoting a more sustainable and holistic approach to managing forest ecosystems.

Tree communication, far from being a rudimentary or passive process, is a dynamic, sophisticated, and essential aspect of forest life. It underpins the resilience, health, and continuity of forests, making trees not just silent sentinels, but active, communicating members of the forest community.

UNDERGROUND NETWORKS - EXPLORING MYCORRHIZAL FUNGI

Deep beneath the forest floor lies a complex, unseen world, an intricate network of mycorrhizal fungi, forming symbiotic relationships with tree roots. This underground network plays a crucial role in tree communication, survival, and overall forest ecology.

The Mycorrhizal Symbiosis

Mycorrhizal fungi form mutualistic associations with tree roots, where the fungi provide the trees with essential soil nutrients, and in return, receive photosynthates from the trees. These mycorrhizal networks comprise continuous fungal mycelia that link multiple plant species, creating a vast, interconnected web. The symbiosis between plants and fungi is a many-to-many relationship, with most fungi acting as broad host generalists.

Ectomycorrhizal and Arbuscular Mycorrhizal Fungi

Mycorrhizal associations are generally classified into two major classes: ectomycorrhizal fungi (EMF) and arbuscular mycorrhizal fungi (AMF). EMF, common in temperate and boreal forests, form symbioses with many tree species, including most conifers and numerous woody shrubs. These fungi are characterized by a mantle that encases the root tip and an extensive network of extramatrical mycelium. AMF, predominant in grasslands, tropical forests, and some temperate trees, are distinguished by the formation of arbuscules within the root cells of their hosts.

Nutrient Exchange and Plant Growth

Mycorrhizal networks are pivotal for the nutrient exchange between trees and fungi. They significantly affect the survival and growth of tree seedlings. In forests dominated by ectomycorrhizal trees, the presence of fungal networks positively influences seedling growth, showcasing a direct benefit of this symbiotic relationship. This growth promotion is attributed to better nutrient acquisition and protection against pathogenic fungi offered by the mycorrhizal networks.

Tree Communication through Mycorrhizal Networks

One of the most remarkable aspects of mycorrhizal networks is their role in tree communication. These networks facilitate the transfer of resources, defense signals, and other biochemicals between trees. The communication through mycorrhizal networks can lead to rapid changes in plant behavior, influencing their physiology, gene regulation, and defense responses. This underground 'tree talk' is essential for the complex adaptive nature of forest ecosystems.

Impact on Forest Ecosystems

The influence of mycorrhizal networks extends to the larger forest ecosystem. They affect the fitness of member plants and fungi, influencing survival, competitive ability, and health. The extent of these networks in the soil is vast, integrating multiple plant and fungal species into a complex adaptive social network. The disruption of these networks can have significant ecological consequences, affecting the resilience and health of the forest community.

Mycorrhizal Networks and Ecosystem Diversity

The dominance of either EMF or AMF in an ecosystem has profound implications for nutrient cycling and carbon sequestration. EMF-dominated forests tend to have lower soil carbon-to-nitrogen ratios, indicating different nutrient cycling regimes compared to AMF-dominated systems. This difference results in more carbon being sequestered in EMF forests, highlighting the ecological importance of mycorrhizal networks.

The Evolution of Mycorrhizal Symbiosis

The mycorrhizal symbiosis is ancient, believed to have facilitated the colonization of land by plants hundreds of millions of years ago. Its evolution is marked by multiple independent occurrences in various plant families. This symbiosis has been a critical factor in the success and proliferation of terrestrial plants, underpinning the diversity and function of present-day ecosystems.

Mycorrhizal networks represent a vital component of forest ecosystems, serving as conduits for communication, nutrient exchange, and mutual support among trees. Their role in tree survival, growth, and forest health underscores the intricate and interdependent nature of life beneath the forest floor.

THE LANGUAGE OF ROOTS - CHEMICAL SIGNALING BELOW GROUND

Beneath the forest floor, a hidden dialogue unfolds, mediated by chemical signaling among tree roots. This subterranean communication, fundamental to forest ecology, encompasses a range of interactions from nutrient exchange to defense strategies.

Root Exudates: The Chemical Messengers

Roots secrete a variety of compounds, collectively known as root exudates. These exudates play diverse roles, from enhancing nutrient uptake to modifying soil properties. They also have biological effects, such as repelling harmful organisms or attracting beneficial ones, thereby influencing the root biome and overall plant fitness.

Chemical Signaling in Symbiosis and Competition

Root exudates act as signaling chemicals in symbiotic interactions, particularly with arbuscular mycorrhizal fungi that colonize roots, facilitating nutrient uptake. These chemical signals are key in establishing and maintaining mutualistic relationships. In competitive scenarios, plants may release allelochemicals that inhibit the growth of neighboring plants, an adaptive strategy for resource allocation.

Plant Defense and Stress Responses

Chemical signaling in roots plays a crucial role in plant defense. When roots detect pathogens or harmful organisms, they can release specific compounds that trigger defense mechanisms. Additionally, under stress conditions such as drought or nutrient deficiency, chemical signals from roots can instigate physiological changes, helping the plant adapt to challenging environments.

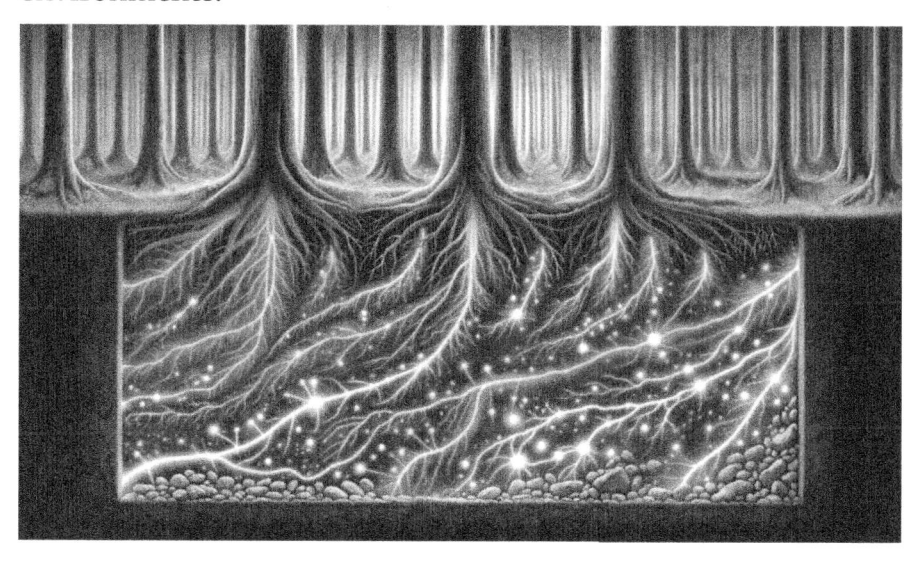

Nutrient Exchange and Soil Health

Root chemical signaling is vital for nutrient exchange, not only within the plant but also in interactions with soil microorganisms. Root exudates can alter the chemical composition of the soil, affecting its health and the availability of nutrients, thus having far-reaching implications for the entire ecosystem.

Root-to-Shoot Communication

Chemical signals from roots are transported to above-ground parts of the plant, influencing various processes. This root-to-shoot signaling can regulate aspects like growth, flowering, and response to environmental cues, ensuring the plant's overall well-being and adaptability.

Chemical Signals and Soil Microbiome

The root microbiome, a complex community of microorganisms living around the root zone, is significantly influenced by chemical signaling. Root exudates can attract beneficial microbes that enhance plant growth and health, while deterring pathogens and harmful bacteria.

Impact on Agricultural Practices

Understanding root chemical signaling has profound implications for agriculture. Manipulating these signals can lead to improved crop resilience, pest management, and soil health, contributing to sustainable agricultural practices.

The language of roots, conveyed through chemical signaling, is a cornerstone of plant communication, essential for survival, adaptation, and interaction with the surrounding environment. This complex, often unseen network of signals plays a pivotal role in maintaining the balance and health of the forest ecosystem.

THE LIFE ABOVE

THE WHISPERING LEAVES - DECODING LEAF SIGNALS

In the canopy of the forest, leaves play a crucial role in tree communication, signaling a myriad of responses to environmental stimuli and internal cues. Let's explore the intricate signaling mechanisms of leaves.

Photosensory Systems and Light Signaling

Leaves are equipped with a photosensory system that enables them to detect changes in light intensity and wavelengths. This system initiates a cascade of signaling that alters gene transcription, influencing plant behavior. For instance, in dense forests, the shade avoidance syndrome (SAS) is triggered in leaves, leading to changes like stem elongation, reduced branching, and early flowering. This response is regulated by multiple photoreceptors and involves interactions between light-responsive genes and transcription factors such as PIF3.

Role of Phytochromes

Phytochromes, present in various organisms including plants, are red and far-red light receptors. In trees, they exist in two forms - the inactive Pr state and the active Pfr state. The balance between these states, influenced by light quantity, color, and temperature, determines the phytochrome response. These light receptors play a pivotal role in regulating plant growth and development in response to light conditions.

Cytokinins in Leaf Development

Cytokinins, a class of phytohormones, significantly influence leaf development. They regulate various processes, such as leaf primordium initiation and shoot apical meristem (SAM) maintenance. The interaction between cytokinins and other phytohormones, like auxins, orchestrates leaf formation and organogenesis. Cytokinins promote cell division in the SAM's organizing center, while auxins are essential for leaf formation. The delicate balance and interaction of these hormones are critical for normal leaf development and growth.

Chemical Responses to Environmental Stimuli

Leaves also play a role in chemical signaling in response to environmental threats. For example, when a deer bites a branch, the tree responds by altering the chemical composition of its leaves, making them less palatable. This ability to distinguish between different types of damage and respond accordingly is a sophisticated aspect of leaf signaling.

Leaf Senescence and Signaling

Leaf senescence, the final stage of leaf development, is regulated by a complex network of signaling pathways. This process involves a transition from nutrient assimilation to remobilization, crucial for the plant's overall fitness. The signaling pathways involved in leaf senescence are influenced by various internal and environmental factors, ensuring the efficient allocation of resources within the tree.

Leaves are not just the site of photosynthesis but also active participants in tree communication. Their ability to sense and respond to light, hormonal cues, and environmental stimuli plays a crucial role in the tree's adaptation and survival strategies. The whispering leaves, through their complex signaling mechanisms, contribute significantly to the dynamic and responsive nature of trees.

THE BREATHING BARK - TREE RESPIRATION AND ITS SECRETS

Tree bark, the protective outer covering of woody plants, plays a crucial role in tree respiration, a vital process for tree survival and growth. Let's delve into the complex functions and mechanisms of tree bark in facilitating respiration.

Bark Structure and Function

Tree bark is an accumulation of several layers outside the vascular cambium, consisting of living tissues like the secondary phloem, which aids in sugar translocation. The outermost layer, known as the rhytidome, is composed of compressed cork cells that provide protection against environmental threats and water loss.

Bark's Role in Tree Respiration

Respiration in trees, including the exchange of gases and metabolic processes, largely occurs through the bark. The bark's structure allows for gas exchange, essential for respiration, while maintaining water balance within the tree. This process is vital for converting stored sugars into energy, crucial for tree growth and maintenance.

Defense Mechanisms in Bark

Beyond its respiratory functions, bark also serves as the first line of defense against various environmental stresses, pathogens, and herbivores. The composition and thickness of bark can vary greatly among tree species, reflecting different evolutionary adaptations to their environments.

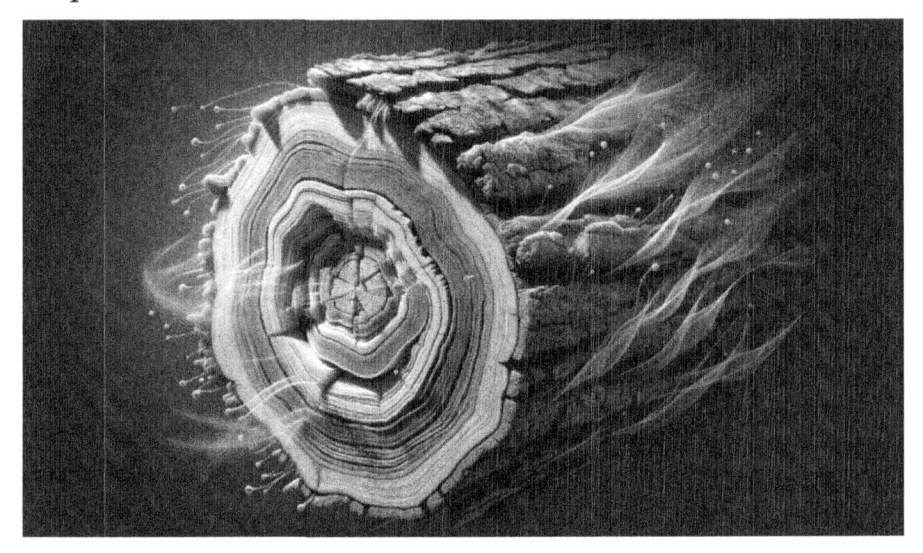

Water and Nutrient Movement

The inner layers of the bark play a pivotal role in the movement of water and nutrients from the leaves to other parts of the tree. This translocation is integral to the tree's overall health and growth, as it ensures the distribution of essential nutrients throughout the tree.

The bark of a tree is not just a protective shield but a complex, multifunctional organ. Its role in respiration, defense, and nutrient translocation underscores its importance in the life of a tree. Understanding the nuances of bark function provides deeper insight into the intricate workings of trees and their adaptation to diverse environments.

FLORAL MESSAGES - FLOWERING AND COMMUNICATION

In the forest ecosystem, flowering is not just a visual spectacle but a complex form of communication within and between tree species. Let's delve into the intricate world of floral messages, exploring how trees use their flowers to communicate.

Chemical Signals in Flowering

Trees use a variety of chemical signals to communicate during the flowering process. These chemicals are released when trees are under attack from pests or diseases, alerting other trees to the danger. This leads to a communal response where neighboring trees produce their own chemical defenses or take other protective measures. For example, some trees release specific chemicals to attract pollinators or to deter herbivores, creating a network of communication based on chemical cues.

Pheromones in Plant Communication

Pheromones, chemicals produced by one organism that affect the behavior or development of another organism of the same species, play a significant role in tree communication during flowering. Trees and plants use pheromones for various purposes, such as attracting pollinators or repelling herbivores. These pheromones are integral to the reproductive success of trees, ensuring effective pollination and the continuation of their species.

Mycorrhizal Networks and Resource Sharing

The communication between trees during flowering is also facilitated by underground networks of mycorrhizal fungi. These networks allow trees to share resources, such as excess sugars, and to communicate warning signals about environmental threats. The mycorrhizal network is vital for the distribution of resources during the crucial period of flowering, supporting the overall health of the tree and the forest.

Vibrations, Sounds, and Light in Communication

Apart from chemical signals and pheromones, trees also communicate through vibrations, sounds, and light. For example, some plants produce specific sounds or vibrations in response to stress or herbivory, which can be detected by other plants. This form of communication enables trees to take preemptive defensive actions. Additionally, some plants use light to communicate, using bioluminescence to send signals to their neighbors.

Flowering in trees is a multifaceted process that involves a wide range of communicative methods. From chemical signals and pheromones to vibrations and light, trees have developed sophisticated ways to communicate during flowering, ensuring their survival and the continuity of the forest ecosystem.

SEASONAL SECRETS

SPRING AWAKENING - TREE RESPONSES TO SEASONAL CHANGE

Spring awakening in trees is a dramatic and critical period, marking the transition from dormancy to active growth. We'll now explore how trees respond to the changing seasons, focusing on the mechanisms and adaptations that enable them to thrive in varying climates.

The Transition from Winter to Spring

The shift from winter to spring is marked by an increase in day length and temperature, signaling trees to end their winter dormancy. Trees have developed several adaptations at the structural and cellular levels to survive the winter and safely transition to spring growth. This includes mechanisms to avoid frost damage and optimize photosynthetic gains once growth resumes.

Phenological Changes

Trees exhibit distinct phenological changes during spring. The expansion of leaves is a critical adaptation, allowing trees to resume photosynthesis and growth. These changes are part of a larger cycle that spans the entire year, with each season playing a vital role in a tree's life cycle. Long-lived trees in temperate climates have evolved to slow their growth during winter to prevent frost damage to new leaves and then resume growth at the appropriate time.

Frost Avoidance and Tolerance Strategies

Apart from leaf expansion, trees employ additional strategies for frost tolerance to protect overwintering parts—buds, wood, roots—during extreme cold. These adaptations are vital for ensuring the health and survival of trees in regions with harsh winters. Each tree species may have evolved different mechanisms to cope with and adapt to long periods of cold temperatures.

Impact of Climate Change on Tree Phenology

Recent studies indicate that climate change is leading to earlier springs and, to some extent, delayed autumns, resulting in longer growing seasons in temperate regions. This shift has implications for primary productivity, carbon capture, and future warming. Trees' phenological responses to climate change are visible and measurable, capturing public interest and aiding in climate change education and engagement.

Interactions with Ecosystems and Climate

Trees' responses to seasonal changes are not isolated events but are deeply interconnected with broader ecosystem processes. The phenological shifts in trees due to climate change impact not only human activities but also conservation efforts, emphasizing the need for integrating phenology into conservation strategies. These shifts play a role in species persistence under changing conditions and must be considered in the context of complex ecosystems.

The spring awakening of trees is a dynamic and intricate process, reflecting a balance between environmental cues and internal biological mechanisms. Understanding these seasonal shifts is essential for comprehending the broader ecological and climatic implications of tree growth and development.

SUMMER'S LUSH CONVERSATIONS - ACTIVE GROWTH AND INTERACTION

Active Growth Phase in Trees

Summer marks a period of vigorous growth and vitality for trees. During this season, trees are in their most active growth phase, driven by longer daylight hours and warmer temperatures. This period of growth is not just about physical expansion; it also involves complex internal processes and external interactions with the environment.

Photosynthesis and Energy Production: With increased sunlight, the rate of photosynthesis escalates. Leaves, now fully unfurled, act as solar panels, capturing light and converting it into chemical energy. This energy is crucial for the tree's growth and the development of new leaves, branches, and, in some species, fruits.

Water Transportation: Summer demands an efficient water transport system to prevent dehydration. Trees draw water from the soil through their roots and transport it to their leaves, a process intensified by the heat. This movement of water, laden with nutrients, is essential for growth and maintaining the tree's structure.

Leaf Adaptations: Leaves may develop adaptations to minimize water loss, such as waxy coatings or smaller leaf sizes. In some species, leaves can change their orientation to reduce exposure to direct sunlight, thus reducing water loss through transpiration.

Interactions with the Environment

Communication with Other Trees: Trees continue to communicate with each other through underground fungal networks. These communications can include the transfer of nutrients to weaker trees or warning signals about pest infestations.

Attracting Pollinators and Reproduction: Flowering trees use the summer to attract pollinators. Flowers with bright colors and alluring scents draw in insects, birds, and other animals, assisting in the process of pollination.

Response to Pests: Trees are more susceptible to pests in the summer. They employ various defense mechanisms, such as producing toxic chemicals or thickening their bark, to deter insects and herbivores.

Interaction with Microbes: The warmer temperatures and increased humidity in summer create a conducive environment for microbial growth. Trees interact symbiotically with these microbes, which play roles in nutrient cycling and root health.

Phenological Changes

Preparing for Fruit and Seed Production: Many tree species start the process of fruit and seed development in summer. This is a critical phase for the propagation of the species and involves the allocation of energy and resources towards the development of seeds.

Adaptations to Heat Stress: Trees also exhibit adaptations to cope with high temperatures. Some may undergo temporary wilting to reduce water loss, while others have specialized bark to reflect sunlight and reduce heat absorption.

Human Interaction

Arboriculture and Pruning: Summer is an important time for tree maintenance. Pruning during this season can be beneficial for shaping the tree and encouraging healthy growth, but it must be done carefully to avoid stressing the tree.

Monitoring for Diseases: With the increase in growth and activity, trees are also more prone to diseases. Regular monitoring and timely intervention can prevent the spread of infections.

Significance for Ecosystems

Role in the Ecosystem: In summer, trees play a pivotal role in their ecosystems. They provide habitat and food for a multitude of species, contribute to the oxygen-carbon dioxide balance, and influence local weather patterns.

Biodiversity Hotspots: Forests and wooded areas become biodiversity hotspots in summer, teeming with life from the microscopic level to large mammals. Each species, from the smallest insect to the largest predator, is interconnected with the life of trees.

Summer represents a time of intense activity and growth for trees. This season is characterized by a bustling interaction of various biological processes, environmental adaptations, and ecological roles. Understanding these dynamics provides insight into the complex and vital role that trees play in our world, not only as individual organisms but as essential components of broader ecosystems.

AUTUMNAL FAREWELLS - PREPARING FOR DORMANCY

Preparing for Dormancy

As autumn arrives, trees begin a remarkable transformation in preparation for the colder months. This process, known as dormancy, is akin to hibernation in animals and is vital for their survival through winter.

Leaf Shedding: Deciduous trees start by shedding their leaves. This is a water conservation strategy, as leaves require and lose a lot of water. By dropping them, trees reduce the risk of dehydration during the dry winter months.

Chemical Changes in Leaves: Prior to falling, leaves undergo chemical changes. Chlorophyll breaks down, causing leaves to lose their green color and reveal autumn's characteristic yellow, orange, and red pigments. This process also involves reabsorbing valuable nutrients from the leaves.

Energy Conservation: With the onset of shorter days and cooler temperatures, trees slow down their growth. This reduction in metabolic activity helps in conserving energy, which is crucial for survival during the low-resource winter months.

Water Movement and Ice Formation: Trees also adapt by altering the way they handle water and ice. They start to move water from their cells to spaces between the cells. This mechanism prevents cells from freezing and bursting, as the formation of ice in these intercellular spaces releases heat, protecting the cells.

Sugar Accumulation: Another adaptation is the accumulation of sugars, proteins, and other substances inside the cells. These act as a natural antifreeze, lowering the freezing point of the cell contents.

Root Growth and Maintenance

Root Development: Interestingly, even when the above-ground parts of a tree are dormant, root systems may continue to grow if the ground temperature is above freezing. This growth is generally slower than in other seasons but is crucial for the overall health of the tree.

Nutrient Uptake: Trees continue to absorb water and nutrients during autumn, although at a reduced rate. This sustenance supports them through the winter and prepares them for the growth spurt in spring.Tree Maintenance in Autumn

Pruning and Care: Autumn is an ideal time for tree maintenance. Pruning can be done more effectively as trees are less susceptible to diseases and pest infestations in their dormant state.

Watering: Providing trees with adequate water before they enter dormancy is crucial, especially for young trees. Deep, infrequent watering is recommended to support root development.

Mulching: Applying mulch around the base of trees in autumn helps to insulate the soil, maintaining a more consistent soil temperature and moisture level.

Protection from Elements: In areas with severe winters, young or fragile trees might require additional protection from extreme cold, snow, and ice.

Ecological Impact

Habitat and Food Source: As trees prepare for dormancy, they become a crucial food source and habitat for wildlife. The seeds, nuts, and fruits produced in autumn provide essential nutrition for birds, mammals, and insects.

Soil Health: The leaf litter from trees enriches the soil with nutrients and provides habitat for numerous microorganisms essential for a healthy ecosystem.

Carbon Storage: During dormancy, trees continue to play a role in carbon sequestration, storing carbon in their wood and roots.

Role in the Ecosystem

Preparing for Spring Regrowth: While dormant, trees are not inactive. They are conserving energy and preparing for the spring, when warmer temperatures and increased light will trigger new growth.

- **Contributing to the Nutrient Cycle**: The process of shedding leaves and slowing growth contributes to the nutrient cycle within the forest ecosystem, laying the groundwork for the next cycle of growth.
- **Supporting Biodiversity**: The changes in trees during autumn have cascading effects on the ecosystem, supporting a wide range of biodiversity.

The process of preparing for dormancy in autumn is a complex and vital phase in the life cycle of trees. It showcases their incredible adaptability and resilience, and the intricate ways in which they interact with and support the broader ecosystem.

THE FOREST ECOSYSTEM

INHABITANTS OF THE CANOPY – INTERACTIONS WITH BIRDS AND INSECTS

Role of Birds in Forest Canopies

Pollination: Birds, especially in regions like New Zealand, play a crucial role as pollinators. Native birds such as the tūī, bellbird, and silvereye are attracted to brightly colored flowers of trees like flax, kōwhai, and tree fuchsia. They transfer pollen from flower to flower while feeding on nectar, thus aiding in the pollination process.

Seed Dispersal: Birds are key agents in seed dispersal for many forest trees. After consuming fleshy fruits, seeds are transported and excreted by birds at locations far from the parent tree. This activity is vital for the regeneration and spread of various tree species. In New Zealand, birds like the kererū, known for its wide gape, are essential for dispersing seeds of larger fruits, thus ensuring biodiversity and forest expansion.

Pest Control: Birds contribute significantly to controlling insect populations in forests. By feeding on harmful insects, they help maintain the ecological balance and protect trees from potential pest infestations.

Insect Dynamics in Forest Canopies

Pollination and Seed Dispersal: Some insects also play a role in pollination. They transfer pollen while feeding on nectar or other parts of the flower. Additionally, certain insects aid in seed dispersal through various mechanisms.

Herbivory and Tree Health: Insect herbivores feed on tree leaves, bark, and other parts, affecting tree health and growth. This interaction can range from being mildly detrimental to severely destructive, depending on the insect species and tree vulnerability.

Mutualistic Relationships: Some insects, such as ants, have mutualistic relationships with trees. They may protect the tree from herbivores or pathogens in exchange for food resources or shelter.

Bird-Insect-Tree Interactions

Tritrophic Interactions: This involves the interaction between three trophic levels: birds (predators), insects (herbivores), and trees (producers). Birds feeding on insects help control herbivore populations, indirectly benefiting the trees.

Influence on Forest Health and Diversity: These interactions influence forest health and biodiversity. Birds and insects, through their various roles, contribute to the structural integrity and functional diversity of forest ecosystems.

Conservation Aspects

Threats to Birds and Insects: Habitat loss, climate change, and pollution pose significant threats to bird and insect populations. This, in turn, impacts their role in forest ecosystems.

Importance of Biodiversity: Maintaining a diverse population of birds and insects is crucial for the health of forest ecosystems. Each species plays a unique role in the ecological balance.

Conservation Efforts: Efforts to protect and conserve bird and insect habitats are essential. This includes preserving old-growth forests, controlling invasive species, and implementing programs like controlled burns to maintain forest health.

The canopy of a forest teems with life, hosting a dynamic interplay of birds, insects, and trees. These interactions are crucial for the functioning and health of forest ecosystems. Understanding and preserving these relationships is vital for the sustainability of forests and the biodiversity they support.

THE FOREST FLOOR - A WORLD BELOW

Composition and Structure

The forest floor, often referred to as the L horizon, is a critical layer in forest ecosystems, mediating between living vegetation above and the soil below. It consists of various forms of plant litter, such as leaf litter, twigs, and branches, which contribute to nutrient cycling. Decomposing organic material forms distinct layers: a top layer of relatively fresh litter (L horizon), an intermediate layer where decomposition is more apparent (F horizon), and a layer of well-decomposed material where original plant residues are no longer recognizable (H horizon).

Role in Nutrient Cycling

The forest floor plays a vital role in the biogeochemical cycle, transmitting nutrients from decaying plant matter to the soil. This process is facilitated by decomposers like fungi, bacteria, and arthropods, which break down organic matter into nutrients that can be reabsorbed by plants. Thus, the forest floor is integral to the sustained productivity and health of forest ecosystems.

Habitat for Organisms

A diverse array of organisms inhabit the forest floor, including insects, fungi, and small mammals. These organisms contribute to the decomposition process and form a complex food web that supports the forest ecosystem. The forest floor also offers habitat for seed germination and growth of various plant species, particularly those adapted to low-light conditions.

Impact on Forest Health

The health of the forest floor affects the overall health of the forest. A healthy forest floor can prevent soil erosion, conserve moisture, and contribute to the forest's resilience against disturbances like forest fires. Conversely, a degraded forest floor can lead to soil degradation and reduced forest productivity.

Variations in Different Forests

The characteristics of the forest floor can vary significantly across different types of forests. In boreal and mountain forests, where decomposition rates are slower, the forest floor tends to be deeper and richer in organic material. In contrast, tropical forests, with their rapid decomposition rates, often have a thinner forest floor layer, except in nutrient-poor soils where decomposition is slower.

Importance in Forest Fires

The forest floor serves as a significant fuel source in forest fires. The accumulation of dry, decomposable material can increase the intensity and spread of fires, impacting forest regeneration and ecosystem dynamics.

Conservation and Management

Despite its importance, the forest floor is often neglected in conservation policy and scientific study. Effective forest management should consider the health of the forest floor to maintain overall forest ecosystem health and productivity. Practices like controlled burns can be used to manage the accumulation of organic material on the forest floor, reducing fire risks and promoting nutrient cycling.

The forest floor is a complex and dynamic component of forest ecosystems, playing critical roles in nutrient cycling, habitat provision, and overall forest health. Understanding and preserving this layer is essential for the sustainable management and conservation of forests.

TREES AND THE CYCLE OF LIFE - DEATH AND REBIRTH IN THE FOREST

Seed and Sprout: The Beginning of Life

The life of a tree begins as a seed, which holds all the necessary nutrients for a tree to form. Different tree species produce seeds that vary in shape and size, adapted to disperse effectively in their environment. For germination, seeds require specific conditions like scarification or cold and moist surroundings. Once these conditions are met, the seed begins to grow roots and sprout, marking the start of a new tree's life.

Seedling and Sapling: The Growth Stages

After sprouting, the tree enters the seedling stage, where it is most vulnerable to diseases, grazing animals, and environmental risks. In this stage, the tree begins to form its primary structure. As it progresses to a sapling, the tree continues to shape itself based on the environmental conditions like light, moisture, and climate variations. This stage is crucial for the tree's survival and future growth.

Adult Tree: Maturity and Reproduction

Once a tree reaches maturity, it can reproduce and produce seeds, continuing the cycle of life. This stage can last for decades or even centuries, depending on the species. Mature trees are integral to the forest ecosystem, providing habitat, food, and maintaining ecological balance.

Old, Declining Tree: The Snag Phase

When a tree reaches the end of its life, it becomes a snag (a standing dead tree). These snags play a vital role in forest biodiversity. They serve as habitat and food sources for various species, including birds, insects, and fungi. The decaying process releases nutrients back into the ecosystem, supporting new growth and maintaining soil health.

Death and Rebirth: The Ecological Impact

The death of a tree is not the end but a transformation. It creates opportunities for new life as it decomposes and returns nutrients to the soil. This process makes room for new plants to grow, allowing more sunlight to reach the forest floor and spurring germination. The decomposing material supports a wide range of organisms, contributing to the forest's biodiversity.

Old-Growth Forests: A Legacy of Life and Death

Old-growth forests are characterized by the presence of trees in all life stages, including saplings, mature trees, dead standing trees, and rotting trees on the forest floor. These ecosystems are crucial for biodiversity and act as a refuge for many species at risk. The presence of dead and dying trees is essential for a healthy forest, providing habitats and influencing its ecological structure.

Conservation and Forest Management

Conservation efforts focus on understanding the complex dynamics of forest life cycles, including patterns of tree death and decay. Managing forests involves mimicking natural processes of succession and disturbance to maintain a balance between growth, death, and rebirth. Forestry practices like logging and controlled burns are used to emulate these natural cycles and keep forests healthy.

Trees and forests undergo a continuous cycle of life, death, and rebirth, each stage contributing to the overall health and vitality of the ecosystem. Understanding and respecting this cycle is crucial for sustainable forest management and conservation.

HISTORICAL WHISPERS

ANCIENT TREES - WITNESSES OF TIME

Ancient trees are remarkable for their longevity and ecological importance. They are life history lottery winners, having survived various environmental changes over centuries, even millennia. Their genetic resilience is a vital evolutionary resource for long-term adaptive capacity in forest ecosystems.

ng

Ecological Role of Ancient Trees

Biodiversity Hotspots: Ancient trees provide unique habitats supporting diverse life forms. They are crucial for many species, including fungi, invertebrates, birds, and mammals.

Carbon Storage: These trees play a significant role in carbon sequestration, helping mitigate climate change effects.

Ecosystem Services: They contribute to ecosystem services such as water regulation, soil stability, and microclimate control.

Genetic Reservoir

Adaptive Traits: Ancient trees carry genes that have enabled them to withstand various environmental challenges. Their genetic diversity is essential for the adaptive capacity of forests.

Seed Dispersal: They produce seeds with a high genetic variability, crucial for the survival and evolution of tree species.

Threats and Conservation

Environmental Changes: Ancient trees are threatened by climate change, habitat destruction, and diseases.

Conservation Efforts: Protecting these trees involves preserving their habitats and understanding their role in ecosystems.

Cultural and Historical Significance: They are also important for their cultural, historical, and aesthetic values.

Ancient trees are not just individual organisms but integral components of their ecosystems. Their preservation is crucial for maintaining biodiversity, ecosystem stability, and genetic diversity, which are vital for forests' long-term health and resilience.

TREES IN MYTH AND LEGEND - CULTURAL SIGNIFICANCE

Trees as Symbolic Entities

In various cultures, trees have been revered as sacred entities, embodying spiritual and cultural values. From ancient mythologies to contemporary literature, trees have been depicted as symbols of life, wisdom, and the interconnectedness of all beings.

Trees in Ancient Mythologies

World Trees: In many mythologies, such as Norse (Yggdrasil) and Hungarian folklore, trees represent the connection between the heavens, earth, and underworld. These cosmic trees symbolize the unity of different realms of existence.

Trees of Life and Death: In Micronesian myths, trees symbolize life and death, echoing the biblical story of Eden with trees that bestow mortality or immortality.

Deity and Spirit Abodes: Trees have been considered as dwellings for gods, spirits, or transformed humans. In Greek mythology, Dryads were nymphs living in trees, dying with them when cut down.

Trees in Folklore and Cultural Beliefs

Trees as Healers: In various cultures, trees have been thought to possess healing powers. Practices like tying cloth pieces to branches or passing sick individuals through tree splits were common for transferring diseases to the tree for healing.

Sacred Trees in Rituals: Trees like the Acacia in Egyptian mythology and the Ash in Celtic lore were central to rituals and worship, seen as bridges to spiritual realms.

Trees in Stories and Literature: In literature, trees have often been depicted as magical and wise beings. J.R.R. Tolkien's mythopoeic tales, for instance, include significant trees that symbolize life, knowledge, and resilience.

Trees as Cultural and Environmental Icons

Trees and Environmental Awareness: The reverence for trees in myths and legends also reflects an early understanding of their ecological importance, such as their roles in sustaining life and balancing nature.

Trees in Modern Narratives: In modern times, trees continue to play symbolic roles in stories, films, and TV shows, often representing nature's power and humanity's connection to the environment.

The cultural significance of trees in myths and legends underscores their importance not just as physical entities but as symbols carrying deep spiritual, ecological, and cultural meanings. This rich heritage of tree symbolism continues to inspire and inform our relationship with the natural world.

HISTORIC TREES - STORIES THEY TELL

Historic trees have witnessed significant events and cultural shifts, standing as silent observers of history. These trees are not just natural wonders but also hold profound stories, marking milestones in human civilization.

Anne Frank's Chestnut Tree - A Symbol of Hope

In Amsterdam, the chestnut tree Anne Frank wrote about in her diary during World War II became a symbol of resilience and hope. Despite its demise in a storm in 2010, saplings from the tree continue to spread its legacy around the world.

Charter Oak - Connecticut's Symbol of Independence

The Charter Oak in Hartford, Connecticut, played a pivotal role in American history. According to legend, the document granting autonomy to Connecticut was hidden within this tree during a confrontation with the British in 1687. The tree, which fell in a storm in 1856, remains a symbol of American independence.

September 11 Survivor Tree - Resilience Amid Tragedy

The Survivor Tree, a callery pear found at Ground Zero after the September 11 attacks, symbolizes survival and resilience. Nursed back to health and replanted at the National September

11 Memorial, it stands as a living tribute to resilience in the face of tragedy.

Major Oak - Robin Hood's Legendary Hideout

The Major Oak in Sherwood Forest, England, is steeped in legend as the hideout of Robin Hood and his merry men. This tree, believed to be over a thousand years old, represents the folklore and history of medieval England.

The Tree of Ténéré - Lone Survivor in the Sahara

In Niger, the Tree of Ténéré was once the most isolated tree on Earth, serving as a vital navigation marker in the Sahara Desert. Its destruction by a drunk driver in 1973 ended its centuries-old role as a guide through the vast desert.

The General Sherman Tree - A Natural Wonder

In California's Sequoia National Park, the General Sherman Tree, a giant sequoia, stands as the world's largest known living single-stem tree. Named after Civil War General William Tecumseh Sherman, it symbolizes the majesty of the natural world.

The Emancipation Oak - A Monument to Freedom

At Hampton University in Virginia, the Emancipation Oak holds a special place in African American history. Underneath this tree, slaves gathered in 1863 to hear the first Southern reading of the Emancipation Proclamation. The tree symbolizes freedom and education for African Americans.

Bodhi Tree - Enlightenment and Spiritual Growth

In Bodh Gaya, India, the Bodhi Tree is where Siddhartha

Gautama, the founder of Buddhism, attained enlightenment. This tree represents spiritual growth and enlightenment in Buddhist traditions.

Historic trees tell stories of hope, freedom, spirituality, and resilience. They are living witnesses to our past, connecting us to moments that have shaped our world. These trees are not just part of our natural heritage but are deeply entwined with our cultural and historical identity.

TREES AND HUMANITY

TREES AND HUMAN HEALTH - THE HEALING POWER OF FORESTS

Physical and Mental Health Benefits

Air Purification: Trees play a crucial role in cleaning the air, particularly in urban environments. They remove pollutants like particulate matter, which arises from fossil fuel combustion and is dangerous to our lungs. Urban trees, especially near highways and factories, can significantly reduce respiratory ailments like asthma and heart disease.

Stress Reduction: Numerous studies have shown that spending time around trees and in forests lowers blood pressure, reduces stress hormones like cortisol and adrenaline, and improves overall mood. This effect is not replicated in treeless urban settings.

Mood Enhancement: Being in greener environments is linked to reduced negative thoughts, fewer symptoms of depression, better reported moods, and increased life satisfaction. Urban areas with more trees see fewer prescriptions for anti-depressants.

Cooling Urban Heat Islands: Trees mitigate the Urban Heat Island effect, especially significant in cities where pavement absorbs heat. A tree's shade acts like natural air conditioning, making urban areas cooler and more habitable.

Healing and Recovery

Faster Recovery from Surgery: Patients with views of trees and greenery from their hospital rooms recover faster, have shorter postoperative stays, take fewer painkillers, and experience fewer complications compared to those with views of walls or no views.

Attention and Cognitive Benefits: Natural environments help alleviate attention fatigue. Children who spend time in nature show a reduction in attention fatigue and related symptoms. This is particularly beneficial for children diagnosed with ADHD.

Community and Economic Health

Economic Benefits: As trees mature, they enhance property values, contributing to stronger neighborhoods and vibrant communities. Higher property values lead to more resources for health care, fresh food, and community services.

Water Filtration: Trees play a vital role in filtering and cleaning water supplies. By absorbing and filtering rainfall, they remove pollutants and sediments, releasing cleaner water into waterways and underground aquifers, reducing the cost and effort required to treat water.

Biodiversity and Ecosystem Services

Wildlife Habitat: Trees provide vital habitats for diverse species. From insects to birds and mammals, they support complex and resilient ecosystems, contributing to the overall health of the environment.

Forest Bathing: The practice of forest bathing (spending time in forested areas) has been shown to have numerous health benefits, including improved immune function, enhanced mental well-being, and increased energy.

The health benefits of trees and forests are multifaceted, impacting physical, mental, and community health. From purifying the air to providing tranquil spaces for recovery and reflection, trees are indispensable allies in promoting human health and well-being.

THE TREES THAT FEED US - FRUIT AND NUT TREES

Fruit and nut trees stand as bountiful pillars in the world's diverse ecosystems, their branches laden with nature's gifts that have nourished civilizations through time. These trees, with their deep roots and far-reaching canopies, are not just providers of sustenance but also pivotal characters in the narrative of our planet's ecological and cultural history.

The journey of fruit and nut trees begins with their remarkable biological adaptations. These trees have evolved to produce a vast array of fruits and nuts, each with its unique size, color, taste, and nutritional profile. The variety is staggering – from the succulent mangoes and apples to the robust walnuts and almonds – each species has adapted to its environment, ensuring its survival and proliferation.

The lifecycle of these trees is a spectacle of nature's rhythms. Each spring, they burst into blossoms, attracting a plethora of pollinators. This phase of flowering and subsequent fruiting is crucial for the survival of not just the trees themselves, but also for the myriad of species that depend on them. The seasonal cycles dictate their growth and dormancy, aligning them intimately with the environment.

Humanity's relationship with fruit and nut trees is as old as civilization itself. These trees have been domesticated and cultivated for thousands of years, playing a central role in agricultural development. Orchards and groves of fruit and nut trees have been a staple in human settlements, a testament to their economic and nutritional importance.

The nutritional value of fruits and nuts is unparalleled. They are rich in vitamins, minerals, fibers, and essential fats, contributing significantly to human health. Beyond mere sustenance, they have medicinal properties and have been used in traditional healing practices across cultures. Their role in contemporary diets continues to be of paramount importance.

Ecologically, fruit and nut trees are vital. They support biodiversity by providing habitats and food for numerous animal species. The role they play in maintaining the health of ecosystems is critical – they improve soil quality, aid in water retention, and contribute to the overall balance of the environment.

Despite their significance, fruit and nut trees face numerous challenges. Climate change, pests, diseases, and the encroachment of human development threaten their survival. The loss of these trees has far-reaching impacts, not just on the environment but also on food security and cultural practices.

Conservation efforts are underway to protect and sustain these vital tree species. There is a growing recognition of the need to preserve traditional varieties and cultivate them using sustainable practices. Research is focused on improving their resilience to environmental stresses and enhancing their yield.

The story of fruit and nut trees is a testament to the interconnectedness of life. These trees do not stand in isolation but are part of a larger ecological and cultural tapestry. They remind us of the delicate balance of nature and the need for stewardship to ensure that they continue to thrive for generations to come.

Fruit and nut trees are not just passive elements in our environment. They are dynamic, living beings that have shaped and been shaped by human history. They continue to feed us, body and soul, and stand as silent witnesses to our changing world, reminding us of the need to live in harmony with nature.

SACRED GROVES - SPIRITUAL AND RELIGIOUS CONNECTIONS

Across cultures and continents, sacred groves have long been revered as the abodes of gods and spirits, places where the natural world intersects with the divine. These groves, often untouched and preserved for centuries, hold not only ecological wealth but also immense spiritual and historical value.

In ancient traditions, sacred groves were considered portals to the spiritual realm. The Druids of Celtic Europe held their rituals in oak groves, considering them sacred. Similarly, in India, the concept of "Dev Van" or "God's forest" is central to many communities, where certain forests are preserved for religious practices and are home to temples and shrines.

The ecological importance of these groves cannot be overstated. Acting as reservoirs of biodiversity, they often harbor species that are rare and endangered. The groves provide a multitude of ecosystem services, including water conservation, soil preservation, and climate regulation. In many cases, these groves are among the last remnants of indigenous vegetation in heavily altered landscapes, making them crucial for conservation efforts.

Sacred trees within these groves, such as the Bodhi Tree under which Buddha is said to have attained enlightenment, or the ancient Yew trees found in English churchyards, are often central to religious narratives and practices. These trees are not just biological entities but symbols of life, wisdom, and continuity, deeply woven into the spiritual fabric of societies.

However, sacred groves face numerous threats in the modern world. Deforestation for agricultural and urban development, along with the erosion of traditional beliefs and practices, has led to the degradation of many such groves. Climate change further exacerbates these threats, altering the delicate balance of these ecosystems.

Despite these challenges, sacred groves continue to be relevant in modern society, serving as vital green spaces and cultural heritage sites. Efforts to revive and protect these groves are being undertaken by various organizations and communities. In urban areas, the concept of sacred groves is being reimagined to create green spaces that serve both ecological and spiritual needs, offering solace and connection to nature amidst the concrete landscape.

Sacred groves stand as a testament to the profound connection between humans and nature, a reminder of the reverence and protection that the natural world deserves. They are not just relics of the past but are vital for the ecological and spiritual health of the present and future generations.

In a world increasingly disconnected from nature, sacred groves offer a bridge to our past, a sanctuary in the present, and a hope for the future. They remind us of the intricate ways in which human life is intertwined with the trees and forests, urging us to recognize the sanctity of all life and the need to protect these precious ecosystems.

TREES OF THE WORLD

RAINFOREST VOICES - THE LUNGS OF THE EARTH

The tropical rainforests, often referred to as the "lungs of the Earth," are remarkable ecosystems that play a crucial role in sustaining life on our planet. Covering a mere 6% of the Earth's surface, they are home to over half of the world's plant and animal species, a testament to their unparalleled biodiversity.

One of the most striking features of rainforests is their immense canopy, a multi-layered expanse that houses a diverse array of flora and fauna. This canopy is not just a physical structure but a dynamic interface where intricate ecological interactions occur. It's a realm where sunlight is transformed into life, fueling the photosynthetic engines of countless tree species.

Beneath the canopy, the understory and forest floor present a world of subdued light and dense vegetation. Here, the trees communicate through a complex network of roots and fungal associations known as mycorrhizae. These networks facilitate the transfer of nutrients and information, playing a vital role in the forest's resilience and health.

Rainforest trees are not solitary entities; they exist in a state of constant interaction with their environment. They provide habitat and food for numerous species, from the tiniest insects to the great apes. The interdependence of these species and their tree hosts is a delicate balance, a symphony of life where each organism has its part to play.

One cannot discuss rainforests without acknowledging their role in climate regulation. Through the process of photosynthesis, these forests absorb vast amounts of carbon dioxide, a greenhouse gas, and produce oxygen. They are pivotal in mitigating climate change, acting as carbon sinks that help balance the Earth's atmosphere.

Rainforests are also reservoirs of genetic diversity, a treasure trove for scientists and researchers. Many of the world's medicines have been derived from the plants found in these forests. Their potential for future scientific discoveries and medical breakthroughs is immense, making their conservation a matter of global health and well-being.

However, these forests face unprecedented threats. Deforestation, driven by logging, agriculture, and mining, is destroying vast swathes of rainforest at an alarming rate. The loss of these forests is not just an environmental issue but a global crisis that affects the climate, biodiversity, and the very air we breathe.

Efforts to conserve and restore rainforests are ongoing, involving a range of strategies from local to global scales. Indigenous peoples, who have been the custodians of these forests for millennia, are at the forefront of many of these efforts. Their traditional knowledge and sustainable practices are invaluable in the fight to save these ecosystems.

The voices of the rainforest are a chorus of life, a reminder of the intricate and inextricable link between humans and nature. These forests are not just distant, green expanses; they are the heart of our planet, vital to our survival and the well-being of countless species. As the lungs of the Earth, their health and resilience are our responsibility, a duty we must uphold for future generations.

ANCIENT BRISTLECONES - THE OLDEST LIVING TREES

Ancient Bristlecone Pines, notably Pinus longaeva, are among Earth's oldest living organisms. These trees, with their twisted and gnarled forms, stand as sentinels of time, surviving in the harsh conditions of high altitudes in the White Mountains of California, Nevada, and some parts of Utah. Growing between 9,800 and 11,000 feet above sea level, they endure in xeric alpine conditions, often in limestone-based soils.

Bristlecone Pines are renowned for their incredible longevity, with some individuals like Methuselah being over 4,800 years old, making them the oldest known non-clonal organisms. Their longevity is attributed to a high ratio of dead to live wood, reducing respiration and water loss. This feature, along with their sectored architecture, allows them to survive even if part of their root system is compromised.

The twisted and weathered appearance of these trees, growing in sparse stands, tells a story of survival against the elements. Typically, they stand 30 feet tall or less but can reach up to 60 feet in more favorable conditions. Their bark is reddish-brown with deep fissures, and the branches are covered with short, bottle-brush-like green needles, which may remain functional for up to 40 years.

The name "bristlecone" derives from the prickly bristle on the immature cones. These cones, initially a deep purple, mature over two years, turning brown and releasing seeds, which are wind-dispersed. The reproductive cycle of these trees is slow, mirroring their overall growth rate.

Bristlecone Pines play a crucial role in dendroclimatology, the study of climate change through tree-ring analysis. By cross-dating millennia-old bristlecone pine debris, researchers have created a continuous record extending 9,000 years into the past. The trees' rings are a window into historical climate conditions, informing about past volcanic eruptions and the progression of human civilizations.

Despite their resilience, Bristlecone Pines face threats from climate change, with rising temperatures affecting high-altitude trees. The Rocky Mountain population is particularly vulnerable to white pine blister rust and mountain pine beetles. Preservation efforts are ongoing, with many habitats like the Inyo National Forest's Ancient Bristlecone Pine Forest being protected.

These ancient trees are more than just biological entities; they are a connection to our planet's past. Walking among these age-old giants, one cannot help but feel humbled and awed. They are a living testament to endurance, standing as witnesses to thousands of years of Earth's history, enduring through climatic and societal changes. The Ancient Bristlecone Pines remind us of the persistence of life and the importance of understanding and preserving these venerable natural wonders.

TREES OF THE SAVANNAH - ADAPTATION AND SURVIVAL

The savannah, a biome characterized by its rolling grasslands and scattered trees, is a testament to the resilience and adaptability of nature. In this environment, trees face extreme conditions – prolonged dry seasons, nutrient-poor soils, and frequent fires. Yet, amidst these challenges, several tree species not only survive but thrive, each adapting in remarkable ways.

Dominant Trees and Their Unique Traits

The savannah's tree population is diverse, with species such as the Acacia, Baobab, and Jackalberry being prominent. Acacias, recognizable by their flat-topped appearance and thorny branches, have developed deep root systems to access water and thick bark to protect against fires. The Baobab, known for its massive, water-storing trunk, can live for thousands of years, providing food and shelter to myriad wildlife. The Jackalberry tree, towering up to 80 feet, thrives on termite mounds, utilizing the aerated soil for better root growth.

Specialized Adaptations for Survival

These trees have evolved to cope with the savannah's harsh conditions. Many species, like the Acacia, have small, waxy leaves to reduce water loss. The Baobab's ability to store water in its trunk is a vital adaptation for surviving the dry season. Additionally, many savannah trees, such as the Umbrella Thorn Acacia, have developed long taproots to reach deep groundwater sources.

Interdependence with Wildlife

Savannah trees play a crucial role in supporting the ecosystem's wildlife. The Acacia, for example, has a symbiotic relationship with certain ant species that protect it from herbivores. The Baobab's fruits are a key food source for animals like elephants and monkeys, while its hollow trunks provide homes for various creatures. The Jackalberry's fruits are a vital food source for birds and mammals.

Unique Species Across Different Savannas

Savannahs around the world host unique tree species adapted to their specific environments. In African savannas, the Sausage Tree and the Yellow Fever Tree are notable. The Sausage Tree produces large, sausage-shaped fruits, and the Yellow Fever Tree is recognized for its yellow bark and role in photosynthesis. In other savannas, like those in Australia, the Gum Tree Eucalyptus and Candelabra Tree are prevalent, each with unique adaptations like fire-resistant bark and water-conserving leaves.

Challenges and Conservation

Despite their resilience, savannah trees face threats from climate change, deforestation, and overgrazing. Their conservation is vital for maintaining the biodiversity and ecological balance of the savannah biome. Efforts are underway to protect these ecosystems through sustainable land management and the creation of protected areas.

The trees of the savannah, with their remarkable adaptations and crucial ecological roles, are a testament to the incredible resilience of nature. They not only provide essential resources for wildlife but also offer insights into surviving and thriving in challenging environments. As symbols of endurance and adaptability, these trees are invaluable components of our global ecosystem.

TREES AND CLIMATE

TREES AND CARBON SEQUESTRATION - FIGHTING CLIMATE CHANGE

Trees play a pivotal role in combating climate change through carbon sequestration, the process of absorbing and storing atmospheric carbon dioxide (CO_2) in their biomass. This natural ability of trees and forests is integral to global efforts to mitigate climate change and maintain the ecological balance.

The Science of Carbon Sequestration

Through photosynthesis, trees absorb CO_2 from the atmosphere and store it in their trunks, branches, leaves, and roots. This process transforms CO_2 into organic carbon, effectively removing it from the atmosphere. The carbon remains stored in the tree for its lifetime, which can span decades to centuries, depending on the species.

Global Impact of Forests on Climate

Forests, especially tropical rainforests, are major carbon sinks, absorbing more CO_2 than they emit. They play a critical role in cooling the planet by more than 1 degree Celsius. The cooling effect of forests extends beyond carbon sequestration.

Trees release water vapor through evapotranspiration, cooling their surroundings. Additionally, uneven forest canopies and the production of aerosols contribute to cooling by reflecting sunlight and seeding clouds.

Challenges and Limitations

However, there are challenges to relying solely on trees for carbon sequestration. One major issue is the availability of land for new tree plantations, as much potential land is currently used for agriculture, industry, and urban development. Moreover, trees are not permanent carbon stores. When trees die, decay, or are burned, they release the stored CO_2 back into the atmosphere. Thus, the protection of existing forests is crucial, as it is more efficient and effective than planting new forests.

Impact of Climate Change on Forests

Climate change itself poses a threat to forests' ability to sequester carbon. In the Western U.S., for example, declining tree growth rates due to decreased precipitation and increased temperatures have weakened the carbon sink capacity of forests. Wildfires, pests, and diseases further exacerbate this issue.

Importance of Conservation and Sustainable Management

The preservation and sustainable management of existing forests are vital. This includes reducing deforestation, preventing forest degradation, and promoting restoration. These actions not only help in carbon sequestration but also preserve biodiversity and maintain ecological balance.

Broader Perspective on Forest Benefits

Forests provide multiple climate-cooling benefits beyond carbon sequestration, such as influencing local climate through evapotranspiration and canopy topography. Therefore, conservation efforts should consider the multifaceted role of forests in the climate system.

Trees and forests are indispensable allies in the fight against climate change, offering a natural solution for carbon sequestration and providing numerous ecological benefits. While they alone cannot solve the climate crisis, their protection and sustainable management are crucial components of a broader strategy to reduce greenhouse gas emissions and combat global warming.

THE IMPACT OF DEFORESTATION - A GLOBAL ISSUE

Deforestation, the large-scale clearing of forested land, poses a significant threat to global ecosystems, climate, and biodiversity. It contributes substantially to climate change, disrupts water cycles, and leads to loss of biodiversity and increased greenhouse gas emissions.

Global Scale and Drivers of Deforestation

Over the past three decades, approximately 420 million hectares of forest have been lost, primarily due to the expansion of agricultural land for cash crops like palm oil, soy, and cattle ranching. This deforestation is not uniform but is particularly concentrated in the humid tropics of Africa, South America, and Southeast Asia.

Impact on Climate Change

Deforestation contributes significantly to global greenhouse gas emissions, accounting for approximately 7-12% of total emissions. This impact is largely due to the carbon stored in forests being released into the atmosphere when trees are cut or burned. For instance, in parts of the Amazon, deforestation and forest fires have turned the region into a net source of carbon emissions, reversing its role as a carbon sink.

Biophysical Effects and Biodiversity Loss

Deforestation has profound biophysical effects on the climate. It alters local climates through changes in albedo, evapotranspiration, and cloud formation. The loss of forests also leads to biodiversity loss. Many species, unable to survive in the remaining forest fragments, face extinction. This loss of biodiversity affects ecosystem services, including pollination, pest control, and disease regulation.

Soil Erosion and Water Cycle Disruption

The removal of trees leads to increased soil erosion, disrupting nutrient cycles and reducing agricultural productivity. Deforestation also affects local and regional water cycles. Without forests to facilitate the process of evapotranspiration, areas experience changes in precipitation patterns and river flow, leading to water scarcity in some regions.

Socio-Economic Impacts

Billions of people rely on forests for livelihood, shelter, water, fuel, and food security. Deforestation disrupts these resources, particularly affecting indigenous peoples and local communities. It can lead to social conflict, migration, and increased vulnerability of rural communities.

Reducing Emissions from Deforestation and Forest Degradation (REDD+)

REDD+ is a policy initiative aimed at reducing emissions from deforestation and forest degradation. It offers financial incentives to developing countries to reduce emissions from forested lands and invest in low-carbon paths to sustainable development. While REDD+ has shown potential in reducing CO_2 emissions, challenges remain in its implementation, including issues of fairness, effectiveness, and the difficulty in monitoring and measuring deforestation rates.

The impact of deforestation is a critical global issue, affecting climate change, biodiversity, water cycles, and human societies. To address this issue effectively, a multifaceted approach is required, including sustainable land use policies, conservation efforts, and initiatives like REDD+. Protecting existing forests and restoring degraded ones are vital steps toward mitigating the adverse effects of deforestation and preserving the ecological balance.

REFORESTATION - HOPE FOR THE FUTURE

Reforestation, the process of replanting trees in deforested areas, is increasingly recognized as a key strategy in the fight against climate change. It offers a nature-based solution to sequester carbon, restore ecosystems, and provide social and economic benefits.

The Role of Reforestation in Climate Mitigation

Reforestation has the potential to capture substantial amounts of carbon dioxide from the atmosphere. In the United States, trees, soil, and wetlands capture around 11% of the nation's emissions annually. By replanting forests, this figure could potentially increase to 21% of net annual emissions. Reforestation initiatives focus on replanting historically wooded areas that have lost their forest cover, thereby restoring the natural carbon sink function of these ecosystems.

Challenges and Opportunities

Despite its potential, reforestation faces several ecological, social, and financial challenges. Funders of reforestation projects are often concerned with operational risks such as tree survival, political risks, and the credibility of monitoring methods. The success of these projects also depends on community engagement and ownership. Ensuring that local communities benefit materially and participate fully is crucial for the effectiveness of reforestation efforts.

Economic and Social Constraints

In Southeast Asia, reforestation efforts are constrained by economic and social factors. The challenge lies in balancing the need for climate mitigation with the socio-economic realities of the region. Investments in reforestation must consider local livelihoods, land tenure, and community involvement to ensure successful and sustainable outcomes.

Reforestation and Sustainable Development

When implemented effectively, reforestation can contribute to sustainable development. It can empower local communities, create jobs, and improve biodiversity. By embracing multiple perspectives, reforestation projects can synergize with sustainable development goals, addressing climate change while benefiting local populations.

Global Efforts and Potential

The potential for reforestation is immense globally, but achieving this potential requires overcoming the challenges of land availability, ecological suitability, and social acceptability. Identifying areas with the highest potential for successful reforestation, and engaging communities in these efforts, is key to realizing the climate mitigation potential of reforestation.

Reforestation represents a beacon of hope in the global effort to combat climate change. It offers a multi-faceted solution, addressing not just carbon sequestration but also biodiversity conservation, ecological restoration, and socio-economic development. The success of reforestation efforts hinges on a comprehensive approach that integrates ecological, social, and economic considerations, ensuring that the restored forests are resilient, beneficial to local communities, and effective in mitigating climate change.

THE SCIENCE OF TREES

UNDERSTANDING TREE BIOLOGY - FROM SEED TO GIANT

The Journey from Seed to Mature Tree

The life of a tree begins as a seed, a miraculous package containing the potential to transform into a towering giant. Seeds vary in size and shape, but each carries the genetic blueprint of its species. When conditions are right, the seed germinates, drawing on its stored energy to send out roots and a shoot. As the shoot breaks through the soil, the seedling begins its journey towards becoming a mature tree.

Photosynthesis: The Engine of Growth

Photosynthesis is the critical process that enables a tree to grow. In this process, leaves absorb sunlight, carbon dioxide, and water to produce carbohydrates, the tree's food, and oxygen as a byproduct. This energy conversion is the foundation of a tree's growth, allowing it to develop its structure, from leaves and branches to trunks and roots.

Tree Anatomy and Function

A tree is a complex organism, each part serving a unique function. The leaves or needles act as solar panels, capturing sunlight for photosynthesis. Flowers produce fruits, nuts, or cones containing seeds for the next generation. The trunk, comprising different layers like the cambium (growth layer), xylem (water transport), and phloem (nutrient transport), supports and nourishes the tree. The roots anchor the tree and absorb water and nutrients from the soil.

Trees grow by adding layers of wood each year, visible as growth rings in the trunk. These rings can tell us about the tree's age and the environmental conditions during its growth. Different tree species have adapted to various environments, from wet tropical rainforests to arid deserts, each with unique adaptations like leaf structure, root systems, and water storage methods.

Reproduction and Seed Dispersal

Reproduction in trees occurs through seeds, which are often contained in fruits or cones. Seed dispersal mechanisms vary, including wind, water, and animals. Some trees, like the maple, have winged seeds, while others, like the coconut, rely on water for dispersal.

Impact of Climate on Growth

Recent studies have shown that tree growth is not solely limited by photosynthesis (carbon source) but also by the rate at which cells can divide and expand (carbon sink). This means that environmental factors like temperature and water availability play a significant role in a tree's growth. In a changing climate, these factors could limit the growth and carbon-sequestering abilities of forests.

Trees in Ecosystems

Trees play crucial roles in their ecosystems. They act as carbon sinks, absorbing and storing carbon dioxide, a greenhouse gas. They regulate the Earth's temperature by releasing water vapor into the atmosphere, forming clouds that reflect sunlight. Trees also provide habitats for countless species, maintain soil health, and are sources of food and resources for humans.

Challenges and Future Research

Understanding tree biology is essential for addressing challenges like deforestation, climate change, and biodiversity loss. Researchers are exploring ways to enhance tree growth and resilience, understanding tree responses to environmental stresses, and developing sustainable forestry practices.

TREE GENETICS - THE BLUEPRINT OF LIFE

The Genetic Complexity of Trees

Tree genetics is a complex and intricate field that delves into the DNA of trees, unraveling the mysteries behind their growth, development, and adaptation. Each tree species has a unique genetic makeup that determines its characteristics - from leaf shape and bark texture to growth rate and resistance to pests and diseases.

Genetic Diversity and Ecosystem Health

Genetic diversity within tree species is crucial for the health and resilience of forests. It enables tree populations to adapt to changing environmental conditions and withstand threats like diseases, pests, and climate change. Studies have shown that tree genetics can significantly influence entire ecosystems, affecting the diversity and functioning of other plant, animal, and microbial communities.

Tree Genetics and Biodiversity Patterns

Recent research has linked tree genetics to continental-scale biodiversity patterns. For instance, a study focused on cottonwood trees found that genetic variation in these trees significantly influences the communities of insects and fungi they support. This suggests that tree genetics plays a critical role in maintaining regional biodiversity and ecosystem health.

Tree Genetics and Reforestation

Understanding tree genetics is vital for effective reforestation and conservation efforts. Planting genetically diverse tree stock is crucial for creating resilient forests. With climate change, there's a shift towards collecting seeds both locally and from regions with climate conditions expected in the future. This approach helps in maintaining local genetic variation while including trees that are better adapted to future climate conditions.

Genetic Adaptation in Forest Ecosystems

Genomic research in trees is expanding, especially with advancements in sequencing technologies. This research is crucial in understanding how trees adapt to their environment. For example, the genetic diversity in European beech populations provides insights into their Quaternary history and future adaptation strategies.

Association Genetics in Forest Trees

Association genetics is another emerging area in tree genetics. It involves studying the genetic variation within species and linking it to variations in traits like cold-hardiness, drought tolerance, and growth rate. Such studies are crucial for breeding programs aimed at improving tree resilience and productivity.

Genetic Variation and Local Adaptation

The local adaptation of trees to their specific environments is a key area of research. This adaptation is often evident in traits related to climate, such as cold tolerance in conifers. Understanding these adaptations is essential for forest management and conservation, especially in the context of rapid environmental changes.

Tree genetics is the blueprint of life for forest ecosystems. It not only shapes the individual characteristics of trees but also has profound implications for ecosystem health, biodiversity, and adaptation to changing climates. Advancements in genomic research and an understanding of genetic diversity are pivotal in conserving and sustainably managing forest resources for future generations.

MODERN RESEARCH - UNCOVERING NEW SECRETS

Advancements in Imaging Technology
In the realm of tree research, advancements in imaging technology have opened new doors. High-resolution ground-penetrating radar, for instance, allows scientists to examine tree root systems without disturbing the soil. This non-invasive technique reveals how roots intertwine and interact with the soil biome, providing a clearer picture of underground tree communication networks. Each discovery here adds to our understanding of how trees share resources and information, a critical aspect of forest ecology.

Tree Communication and Climate Adaptation
Recent studies have focused on how trees communicate to adapt to changing climates. Researchers have found that certain tree species can share information about environmental stressors, like drought or pests, through biochemical signals. This communication enables neighboring trees to preemptively activate defense mechanisms, a survival strategy that could be key in helping forests adapt to the rapidly changing climate. Understanding these adaptive mechanisms is vital for developing conservation strategies.

Genome Sequencing and Genetic Diversity

The sequencing of tree genomes has been a significant leap forward. By decoding the genetic material of various tree species, scientists can now understand the genetic basis of traits like drought tolerance, disease resistance, and lifespan. This knowledge is crucial for conservation, as it helps identify genetically diverse and resilient populations, ensuring the long-term survival of species in changing environments.

Tree Aging and Longevity Studies
Longevity studies in trees have uncovered fascinating insights into aging processes. Scientists are exploring why some tree species, like the ancient bristlecone pine, live for thousands of years, while others have much shorter lifespans. Understanding the cellular and molecular mechanisms behind tree aging can provide clues about longevity and healthspan in other species, including humans.

Urban Forestry Research
Urban forestry research has gained momentum, focusing on the role of trees in urban environments. Studies show that urban trees contribute significantly to reducing air pollution, mitigating urban heat islands, and enhancing mental health.

Researchers are also exploring the best practices for urban tree planting and maintenance, ensuring that urban forests thrive and provide maximum ecological and social benefits.

The Role of Trees in Ecosystem Services

Trees play a vital role in ecosystem services, and recent research has aimed to quantify this. By evaluating processes like carbon sequestration, water filtration, and biodiversity support, scientists can better argue for the conservation and expansion of forested areas. This research is critical in policy-making, emphasizing the need to preserve and expand green spaces for environmental and human health.

Technological Integration in Tree Health Monitoring

Technological advancements, such as satellite imagery and drones, are being used to monitor tree health on a large scale. These technologies enable the detection of diseased or stressed trees over vast areas, providing crucial data for forest management. This wide-scale monitoring is particularly important in the face of global challenges like invasive species and climate change.

Collaborative International Research Initiatives

Finally, international collaborative efforts are key in tree research. Global challenges like climate change and deforestation require a united approach. Through collaborations, researchers share knowledge, resources, and methodologies, fostering a comprehensive understanding of trees and forests worldwide.

New Methodologies in Tree Research

Innovative methodologies are reshaping tree research. For example, isotope analysis is being used to track water and nutrient movement within trees, revealing how they respond to environmental changes. Additionally, acoustic monitoring techniques are uncovering the sounds of tree growth and stress, providing a unique perspective on tree health and behavior.

Impact of Climate Change on Tree Physiology

Understanding the impact of climate change on tree physiology is a key focus area. Studies are examining how increased CO_2 levels, temperature changes, and altered precipitation patterns affect photosynthesis, growth rates, and reproductive cycles in trees. This research is crucial for predicting how forests will fare in a changing climate and for developing strategies to mitigate negative impacts.

Future of Forest Conservation Efforts

Looking ahead, the future of forest conservation is intertwined with the advancements in tree research. Conservation efforts are increasingly data-driven, leveraging research findings to protect and restore forests effectively. For instance, genetic studies guide the selection of tree species for reforestation projects, ensuring genetic diversity and resilience. Similarly, insights from urban forestry research are shaping the development of green spaces in cities, balancing urbanization with ecological preservation.

Collaboration with Indigenous Knowledge

There's a growing recognition of the importance of integrating indigenous knowledge with modern research. Indigenous communities have long understood the intricate relationships within forests. By combining this traditional knowledge with scientific research, a more holistic understanding of forest ecosystems is achieved. This collaboration is proving invaluable in conservation efforts, ensuring they are culturally respectful and ecologically sound.

Use of AI and Machine Learning in Forestry

Artificial intelligence and machine learning are emerging as powerful tools in forestry research. These technologies are being used to analyze vast amounts of data from satellite images, sensor networks, and forest inventories. This analysis helps in predicting forest growth, assessing fire risks, and monitoring biodiversity. The integration of AI in forestry represents a significant step forward in managing and understanding forests at a global scale.

Public Engagement and Citizen Science

Finally, there is an increasing emphasis on public engagement and citizen science in tree research. Programs that involve the public in data collection and monitoring efforts not only expand research capabilities but also raise awareness about the importance of trees and forests. These initiatives foster a deeper connection between people and nature, crucial for the long-term sustainability of conservation efforts.

Modern research in tree science is a dynamic and evolving field, incorporating advanced technologies and methodologies to deepen our understanding of trees and forests. From genetic studies to AI-driven analytics, these research efforts are crucial for the conservation and sustainable management of forest ecosystems worldwide.

THREATS TO TREES

DISEASE AND PESTS - CHALLENGES FACED BY TREES

Emergence of New Tree Diseases

The global tree crisis is exacerbated by the emergence of new diseases, which are accumulating rapidly. Research landscape ecologists have noted that the number of emerging diseases has doubled approximately every 11 years. Pines, oaks, and eucalypts are among the tree species most impacted by these new diseases, partly due to their wide native distribution in the Northern Hemisphere. Europe leads in the total accumulation of new diseases, with North America and Asia closely following. These diseases pose a severe threat to tree populations globally and are likely to continue impacting trees into the future.

Common Tree Diseases

Some prevalent tree diseases include:

Cedar-Apple Rust: Causes yellow-orange spots on leaves and fruit, leading to premature dropping.

Diplodia Tip Blight: Common on stressed conifers, particularly Austrian pine, it stunts new growth and turns it yellow, then brown.

Dothistroma Needle Blight: Causes pine needles to turn brown at the tips and eventually fall off.

Fire Blight: Affects fruit trees, causing branches to appear scorched and leaves to blacken.

Oak Wilt: A fatal fungal disease for oak trees, leading to rapid wilting and browning of leaves.

Powdery Mildew: Identified by a powdery white coating on foliage, causing leaves to distort and drop.

Phytophthora Root Rot: Attacks trees on poorly drained sites, leading to drought-stressed appearance.

Impact on Carbon Sequestration

Forests play a critical role in capturing carbon from the atmosphere. However, native and non-native insects and diseases impact an average of 50 million acres annually in the U.S., reducing the forests' ability to combat climate change. The emerald ash borer, Dutch elm disease, and invasive shothole borers are among the most damaging, killing millions of trees and reducing carbon sequestration capabilities.

Prevention and Management Strategies

Preventive measures are crucial in managing these diseases and pests. These include:

- Regular watering, especially during droughts.
- Pruning dead or diseased branches to promote new growth.
- Mulching to retain moisture and protect against extreme temperatures.
- Fertilization to provide essential nutrients.
- Pest management for common pests such as aphids, borers, and caterpillars.
- Professional tree inspections for early signs of

disease or damage.

Regional Specificity of Tree Diseases
Different regions have specific diseases that pose significant threats. For instance, in Indiana, prevalent diseases include Dutch Elm Disease, Oak Wilt, Anthracnose, and Apple Scab. These diseases can cause severe damage and even death if not addressed promptly.

Tree Removal as a Last Resort
Despite best efforts, sometimes tree removal is necessary due to severe disease, storm damage, or structural changes in landscaping. Consulting with a professional arborist is recommended to assess the situation and provide expert advice.

The health and longevity of trees are under constant threat from a variety of diseases and pests. Understanding these challenges and implementing proper care and maintenance strategies are crucial for preserving tree health and the benefits they bring to our ecosystems.

Role of Climate Change in Exacerbating Tree Diseases
Climate change is intensifying the spread and severity of tree diseases. Rising temperatures and altered precipitation patterns create favorable conditions for many pathogens and pests.

Stress from drought and heat makes trees more vulnerable to diseases and pest infestations. For instance, drought-stressed trees are more susceptible to attacks by bark beetles and other borers.

Climate change also assists in the spread of diseases and pests to new regions, where native trees may not have natural defenses against these invaders.

Strategies for Building Resilience Against Tree Diseases and Pests

Developing and planting disease-resistant tree varieties is a key strategy. Genetic research and breeding programs are focused on creating trees that can withstand specific diseases or pest infestations.

Integrated pest management (IPM) techniques, combining biological, cultural, and chemical methods, are effective in controlling pest populations without harming the environment.

Enhancing biodiversity in forests can reduce the spread and impact of diseases and pests. A diverse ecosystem is more resilient and less likely to experience widespread devastation from a single disease or pest outbreak.

Importance of Monitoring and Early Detection

Monitoring forests using technologies like satellite imagery and drones helps in the early detection of disease and pest outbreaks. This allows for timely interventions to control the spread.

Citizen science initiatives, where the public reports signs of tree diseases or pest infestations, play a crucial role in early detection and management.

Collaborative Efforts in Managing Tree Health

Global cooperation is essential in addressing the spread of tree diseases and pests. Sharing knowledge, resources, and strategies can lead to more effective solutions.

Partnerships between government agencies, research institutions, conservation organizations, and the public are crucial for developing and implementing successful management strategies.

Adapting Forestry Practices for Future Challenges

Forest management practices must adapt to the changing dynamics brought about by climate change and the emergence of new diseases and pests.

Practices such as selective logging, controlled burns, and maintaining appropriate tree density can help in maintaining forest health and resilience.

Reforestation efforts should consider the future climate and potential disease and pest risks, choosing species and varieties accordingly.

The health and longevity of trees are under increasing threat from a complex interplay of diseases, pests, and environmental changes. Addressing these challenges requires a multifaceted approach that combines scientific research, proactive management, and global collaboration. Ensuring the health of our forests is not just about preserving trees; it's about maintaining the balance of entire ecosystems and the benefits they provide to our planet.

HUMAN IMPACT - URBANIZATION AND ITS EFFECTS

Urbanization's Direct Impact on Forests
Urbanization, especially in regions like Southeast U.S., poses a significant threat to forests. As urban areas expand, they encroach on preserved areas and divide forests into smaller fragments. This fragmentation exposes forests to various stresses such as high temperatures, pollution, and invasive species, thereby impacting their health and biodiversity.

Effects on Urban Trees and Forest Ecosystem Services
Urban trees play a vital role in improving air quality, mitigating heat islands, and enhancing biodiversity. Despite facing challenges like soil degradation and reduced mycorrhizal associations, urban forests can support diverse plant and animal life. They are crucial in carbon sequestration, offsetting some of the carbon emissions from cities.

Heat and Pollution Stress
Trees in urban areas are subjected to higher temperatures and pollution stress. This can lead to decreased growth rates, increased susceptibility to diseases, and reduced ability to perform ecosystem services like air purification and cooling.

Urban Tree Planting and Its Benefits
Investing in urban tree planting has shown to have significant returns on investment (ROI), particularly in terms of heat and particulate matter (PM) reduction. Cities like Jakarta and Atlanta have demonstrated the benefits of strategic tree planting in reducing temperature and improving air quality.

Role in Biodiversity Conservation
Urban forests are increasingly recognized for their role in biodiversity conservation. They provide habitat for various species and contribute to ecological connectivity in urban landscapes. However, more research is needed to understand how urbanization affects forest quality for different plants and animals.

Challenges in Urban Forest Management
Managing urban forests presents unique challenges, including dealing with tree pests and invasive species. The US Fish and Wildlife Service and other organizations are focusing on understanding these challenges to improve urban forest management and conservation.

Climate Change and Urban Trees
Climate change exacerbates the challenges faced by urban trees, including increased temperatures and extreme weather events. Urban trees can play an essential role in climate change adaptation strategies by providing cooling effects and reducing energy demands for air conditioning.

Socioeconomic Benefits of Urban Forests
Urban forests offer numerous socioeconomic benefits, including improving mental health, providing recreational spaces, and enhancing the overall livability of urban areas. The positive

effects of biodiversity and green spaces on the well-being of individuals are well-documented.

Future Directions for Urban Forestry

As urbanization continues, the importance of urban forests is expected to grow. Future urban planning needs to incorporate green infrastructure and tree planting as key components. This includes fostering tree health, ensuring species diversity, and integrating trees into the urban design for maximum ecosystem service provision.

Urbanization poses significant challenges to trees and forests, but it also presents opportunities to enhance urban biodiversity, improve air quality, and mitigate climate change impacts. Strategic urban forest management and planning are imperative to maintain and enhance the ecological and social benefits provided by trees in urban environments.

Enhancing Urban Forest Resilience

Resilience in urban forests can be enhanced through the selection of diverse and locally adapted tree species. This diversity ensures that urban forests can withstand various environmental stresses and pest outbreaks.

Implementing green infrastructure, like green roofs and walls, can complement urban trees in providing ecosystem services and improving urban biodiversity.

Soil management and the use of mycorrhizal inoculants can improve tree health in urban environments where soil conditions are often suboptimal.

Community Engagement in Urban Tree Conservation

Community involvement is crucial for the success of urban forestry initiatives. Educational programs and citizen science projects can raise awareness about the importance of urban trees and engage the public in their conservation.

Community-based tree planting and maintenance programs can foster a sense of ownership and stewardship among urban residents, leading to better care and protection of urban trees.

Role of Policy and Urban Planning

Urban planning and policies should prioritize the integration of green spaces into city landscapes. This includes the creation of urban parks, green corridors, and ensuring that new developments include sufficient tree cover.

Policies that regulate urban development and land use can help prevent the unnecessary loss of trees and forested areas due to urban expansion.

Technological Innovations in Urban Forestry

Technological advancements, such as remote sensing and GIS, are increasingly being used to monitor and manage urban forests, helping in the identification of stressed trees, tracking tree growth, and planning urban green spaces.

Smart city initiatives can include urban forestry as a key component, leveraging technology for efficient water and soil management, and monitoring tree health.

Future of Urban Forests in Global Urbanization

As urbanization continues, the role of urban forests in mitigating its negative impacts becomes increasingly significant. Urban forests are essential for making cities sustainable and livable.

The challenge lies in balancing urban development with the conservation and enhancement of urban green spaces. This requires a collaborative approach involving urban planners, environmental scientists, policymakers, and the community.

Adapting to Climate Change

Urban forests will play a crucial role in helping cities adapt to the effects of climate change, such as increased temperatures and extreme weather events.

Strategies like planting heat-tolerant tree species and creating heat relief zones in cities can help mitigate the urban heat island effect and enhance urban climate resilience.

Sustainable Urban Forest Management

Sustainable management of urban forests involves regular monitoring, maintenance, and adaptation to changing urban conditions.

Incorporating urban forestry in local and national climate action plans can ensure the sustainable management and expansion of urban green spaces.

Urbanization presents both challenges and opportunities for tree conservation. With strategic planning, community involvement, and sustainable management practices, urban forests can thrive and continue to provide vital ecological, social, and economic benefits in an increasingly urbanized world.

CONSERVATION EFFORTS - PROTECTING OUR TREE HERITAGE

Comprehensive Threat Assessment for U.S. Trees

A recent study, involving organizations like The Morton Arboretum and NatureServe, completed the first comprehensive threat assessment for all native tree species in the U.S. This study identified extinction risk, geographic and taxonomic diversity, and leading threats to these species. Notably, oaks and hawthorns have the most threatened species in the U.S. This assessment is crucial for focusing conservation efforts by federal agencies, public gardens, and conservation organizations.

Global Tree Species at Risk

Globally, over 17,000 tree species are at risk due to rapid changes, including deforestation and climate change. The highest rates of tree cover decline are linked to human land use changes and environmental factors. This widespread threat necessitates accurate species extinction risk assessments to identify species requiring urgent conservation attention.

Policy Proposals for Tree Restoration in the U.S.

The U.S. has seen several policy proposals aimed at tree conservation, such as the Climate Stewardship Act, which expands support for tree restoration on private and public lands. This act includes directives for reforestation and establishes a grant program for urban forestry, aiming to plant over 100 million trees in urban areas, particularly in underserved communities.

Arbor Day Foundation's Reforestation Efforts
The Arbor Day Foundation is scaling its efforts to plant 500 million trees by 2027 in areas most in need. This initiative focuses on planting trees globally with a science-based approach, emphasizing the need for community involvement and education in tree planting and conservation.

Restoration of Federal Lands
The REPLANT Act proposes removing the cap on the Reforestation Trust Fund, making more funds available for reforestation on federal lands. This act could address a significant portion of the reforestation backlog in the U.S. and is complemented by other legislation aiming to accelerate tree restoration on private lands.

International Conservation Efforts
The Trillion Trees and Natural Carbon Storage Act focuses on setting targets to increase carbon removal in U.S. forests and other ecosystems, directing agencies to monitor carbon in these areas. The act also emphasizes U.S. climate leadership abroad, promoting conservation and restoration programs as part of international assistance efforts.

Technological and Scientific Advancements
Technological advancements are playing a crucial role in tree conservation. High-tech nurseries and remote sensing data are

being used to support reforestation needs and expand the capacity to produce seedlings. Scientific research is also vital in understanding the carbon impacts of harvested wood products and ecosystem health.

Local and Community-Led Conservation Initiatives

Local and community-led conservation initiatives are crucial for effective tree conservation. These initiatives range from urban forestry programs to community tree recovery and energy-saving tree projects, emphasizing the importance of trees in local ecosystems and communities.

Challenges and Future Directions

The future of tree conservation faces several challenges, including the need for expanded workforce development and sufficient seedling production for large-scale reforestation. Collaborative efforts between government agencies, non-profit organizations, and local communities are essential for addressing these challenges and ensuring the effective conservation of tree heritage.

Protecting our tree heritage requires a multifaceted approach, combining comprehensive scientific assessments, policy interventions, community involvement, and technological advancements. These efforts are vital for preserving biodiversity, mitigating climate change, and sustaining the myriad benefits that trees provide to ecosystems and human societies.

Incorporating Indigenous Knowledge in Tree Conservation

Indigenous knowledge plays a pivotal role in tree conservation. Indigenous practices, honed over centuries, offer invaluable insights into sustainable forest management and biodiversity conservation.

Collaborative efforts that integrate indigenous knowledge with modern conservation science can lead to more effective and culturally respectful conservation strategies.

Protecting Ancient and Rare Tree Species

Conservation efforts prioritize ancient and rare tree species, recognizing their unique ecological and cultural significance. These trees serve as vital genetic reservoirs and are often key to ecosystem stability.

Programs like The Morton Arboretum's Global Tree Conservation Program focus on protecting and restoring vulnerable and threatened trees, including those extinct in the wild.

Expanding Ex-Situ Conservation Efforts

Ex-situ conservation, such as seed banks and botanical gardens, provides an insurance policy against extinction. It ensures the survival of threatened tree species outside their natural habitats.

Efforts are underway to increase the representation of threatened tree species in these collections, especially those not currently conserved in any ex-situ collection.

Global Tree Assessment and Data Sharing

Initiatives like the Global Tree Assessment are crucial for gathering comprehensive data on tree species worldwide. This data informs conservation priorities and strategies.

Establishing a data-sharing methodology among conservation organizations enhances efficiency and collaboration in global tree conservation efforts.

Community Forestry and Urban Tree Conservation

Community forestry programs empower local communities to manage and protect forest resources sustainably. These programs often combine livelihood improvement with conservation goals.

Urban tree conservation initiatives focus on enhancing urban biodiversity and providing ecosystem services in city environments, particularly in underserved communities.

The Role of Policy in Tree Conservation

Policies at national and international levels play a significant role in tree conservation. Legislation like the Climate Stewardship Act in the U.S. and similar policies globally are vital for advancing tree restoration and conservation efforts.

International agreements and collaborations are essential for addressing transboundary conservation challenges and promoting sustainable forestry practices globally.

Technology and Innovation in Conservation

Technological innovations, such as remote sensing and genetic engineering, are increasingly being used in tree conservation, offering new ways to monitor forest health and enhance the resilience of tree species.

Research on tree genetics and breeding programs for disease-resistant and climate-adapted trees is critical for future conservation efforts.

Future Prospects and Challenges

The future of tree conservation faces challenges such as climate change, habitat destruction, and the spread of invasive species. Addressing these challenges requires global cooperation and innovative solutions.

Despite these challenges, there is growing recognition of the importance of trees in maintaining biodiversity, mitigating climate change, and sustaining human well-being.

Tree conservation is a multifaceted endeavor that requires collaboration across scientific disciplines, policy sectors, and communities worldwide. By combining traditional knowledge, scientific research, and innovative policy solutions, we can effectively protect and restore our global tree heritage for future generations.

ARTISTIC EXPRESSIONS

TREES IN ART AND LITERATURE - INSPIRATIONAL MUSES

Trees and Their Representations in Literature and Arts

Trees have been a recurring theme in literature and arts, often symbolizing life, growth, and nature's cycles. They are used to express various concepts such as identity, ethnicity, and nationality. Literary works frequently explore the metamorphosis of humans and non-humans into trees, or the creation of new species versus the extinction of existing ones.

Dendrocommunication in Literature

The concept of dendrocommunication, or the Wood-Wide-Web, has been explored in literature, reflecting on the interconnectedness of trees and their ability to communicate. This theme represents a blend of science and fiction, expanding our understanding of the natural world.

Memorial Trees in History and Culture

Trees serve as symbols of historical and naturecultural memory. In literature and art, they are often depicted as witnesses to history, embodying the passage of time and the continuity of life.

Trees in Poetry

Poets like Robert Frost have immortalized trees in their works. Frost's "Birches" is a classic example, where birch trees are not only a part of the landscape but also a symbol of life's rhythms and a medium for human interaction with nature.

Arborsculpture: The Art of Tree Shaping

Arborsculpture, the art of shaping living trees, is a unique intersection of art and horticulture. Pioneered by Axel Erlandson, it involves manipulating trees into artistic shapes and structures. This form of artistry is a testament to the flexibility and resilience of trees, as well as human creativity in harmonizing with nature.

Living Architecture and Urban Design

The integration of living trees into architectural and urban design, as exemplified by architect Ferdinand Ludwig's Baubotanik (Living Plant Constructions), showcases the potential of trees in sustainable urban planning. His work includes living structures such as a willow tower and a bird-watching station, highlighting the possibility of trees as functional and aesthetic elements in cities.

Ecology in Living Design

Living tree structures continue to provide ecological benefits such as combating soil erosion, producing oxygen, and serving as carbon sinks. This approach to architecture and design emphasizes a symbiotic relationship between humans and nature, moving towards sustainable and balanced living.

Cultural Significance of Trees

Throughout history, trees have been revered and symbolized in various cultures. Their depictions in art and literature reflect humanity's deep-rooted connection with nature and the environment. This cultural significance underscores the importance of preserving trees and forests.

Trees have inspired artists and writers for centuries, serving as symbols of strength, growth, and resilience. Their presence in art and literature is a reminder of the intricate relationship between humans and the natural world, and the importance of preserving this connection for future generations.

Evolution of Tree Representations in Contemporary Literature and Art

Contemporary literature and art have increasingly focused on trees not just as background elements but as central characters or symbols, often highlighting environmental concerns and the human-nature relationship.

The emergence of eco-criticism in literature has led to a deeper exploration of trees, forests, and their ecological and symbolic significance, reflecting the growing environmental awareness in society.

Trees in Myth and Folklore

In myth and folklore, trees often hold sacred or magical significance. They are depicted as living entities with spirits or as gateways to other worlds. These cultural narratives underscore the respect and reverence that various cultures have historically held for trees.

Art and literature continue to draw inspiration from these ancient myths, reinterpreting them in contemporary contexts and exploring their relevance in modern society.

Environmental Awareness and Artistic Depictions

The rise of environmental awareness has influenced the way trees are depicted in art and literature. Artists and writers are increasingly using trees to comment on issues like climate change, deforestation, and biodiversity loss.

This trend reflects a collective consciousness about the environmental crisis and the role of trees in mitigating its effects, as well as a recognition of their intrinsic value beyond utilitarian purposes.

Interdisciplinary Approaches in Tree-Themed Art and Literature

Interdisciplinary approaches, combining science, art, and literature, are enriching the representation of trees. These collaborations lead to innovative expressions and a deeper understanding of trees' ecological and cultural roles.

Literary works and art installations often incorporate scientific concepts like dendrochronology or the Wood-Wide-Web, blending factual knowledge with creative imagination.

Trees as Symbols of Resilience and Hope

In contemporary narratives, trees often symbolize resilience, hope, and the enduring power of nature. They are portrayed as beacons of stability and renewal amidst the changing world.

This symbolism is particularly poignant in the context of climate change and environmental degradation, offering a hopeful perspective on the possibility of regeneration and coexistence with nature.

The Future of Trees in Art and Literature

The representation of trees in art and literature is likely to continue evolving, reflecting the changing relationship between humans and the natural world.

As global environmental challenges intensify, trees will remain powerful symbols and subjects in artistic and literary works, inspiring action, reflection, and a deeper appreciation of the natural world.

Trees in art and literature are not just aesthetic subjects but powerful symbols and storytellers. They bridge the gap between the human and natural worlds, reminding us of our interconnectedness with nature and our responsibility to protect and cherish it.

PHOTOGRAPHY AND TREES - CAPTURING THEIR ESSENCE

Computational Photography and Trees

Computational photography, leveraging algorithms and processing techniques, allows photographers to capture unique and breathtaking images of trees. This includes high-resolution images that reveal intricate details of tree textures, patterns, and the play of light and shadow on leaves and branches.

VR and AR in Tree Photography

Virtual reality (VR) and augmented reality (AR) photography offer immersive experiences of tree environments. This technology can transport viewers to virtual forests or overlay digital information about tree species and ecosystems onto real-world scenes.

Drone Photography of Forests

Drone photography provides aerial perspectives of forests, capturing the vastness and diversity of tree canopies. These images offer a new understanding of forest landscapes, showcasing their beauty and ecological importance from above.

High Dynamic Range (HDR) Imaging of Trees

HDR imaging captures the full range of tones in tree environments, from the brightest sunlight filtering through leaves to the deepest shadows in forest undergrowth. This technique creates images with enhanced dynamic range, revealing the rich textures and colors of trees in different lighting conditions.

3D Tree Photography

3D photography of trees adds depth to traditional images, allowing viewers to explore and interact with trees in a more engaging way. This could include 3D models of rare or ancient trees, providing a virtual experience of their size and structure.

Advanced Post-Processing of Tree Images

Post-processing software enables photographers to enhance tree photos with intelligent auto-enhancement, content-aware fill, and non-destructive editing. These tools transform tree photographs into artistic representations, emphasizing their beauty and ecological significance.

Next-Generation Camera Sensors for Tree Photography

Advanced camera sensors capture more detail in tree photography, enhancing colors and dynamic range. This technology is essential for capturing the intricate details of trees in varying lighting conditions, from dense forests to solitary trees in open landscapes.

Instant Printing and Sharing of Tree Photos

Instant printing and sharing technologies allow photographers to share their tree images in real-time, fostering a global appreciation for trees and their environments. This includes printing physical copies of memorable tree scenes or uploading images to social media.

Storytelling Through Tree Photography

Photographers use trees to tell compelling stories, exploring themes of growth, resilience, and the interplay between humans and nature. Self-portraits and documentary-like images featuring trees can convey personal narratives and broader environmental messages.

Cinematic Tree Photography

Cinematic photography applies filmmaking artistry to tree images, creating dramatic compositions with bold colors and depth of field. This style captures the majestic and often ethereal nature of trees, making them appear as if stills from a movie.

High Contrast and Experimental Tree Images

High contrast and experimental photography techniques create visually striking tree images. These methods play with light, shadows, and textures, highlighting the dramatic and sometimes surreal aspects of trees and forests.

The convergence of advanced photography techniques and technology has transformed how we capture and perceive trees. From computational photography to cinematic styles, these innovations offer new perspectives on trees, deepening our understanding and appreciation of these vital natural elements.

Pattern-Focused Tree Photography

Photography focusing on patterns and textures in trees highlights their diverse and often overlooked aspects. These images capture the intricate designs of bark, the symmetry of leaves, and the unique patterns found in branches and roots.

This trend encourages photographers to capture semi-abstract looks, turning ordinary tree scenes into captivating works of art.

Golden Hour Lighting in Tree Photography

The golden hour, the time just after sunrise or before sunset, offers perfect lighting conditions for tree photography. This natural light enhances the colors of leaves and bark, creating warm, glowing images that highlight the beauty of trees.

Photographs taken during the golden hour capture the serene and tranquil essence of tree landscapes, making them more appealing and emotionally resonant.

Rustic Backgrounds in Tree Photography

Rustic backgrounds, such as wood grains, stumps, or natural landscapes, provide a harmonious and appealing setting for tree photography. These natural elements enhance the organic feel of the images.

Using rustic backgrounds allows photographers to focus on the key elements of the photo while maintaining a connection with nature, which is particularly effective in tree photography.

High Drama in Tree Images

High drama photography includes striking color contrasts, super close zooms, and emphasized natural elements. This style creates visually impactful images that capture the majestic and sometimes dramatic nature of trees.

This trend emphasizes the grandeur and scale of trees, evoking a sense of awe and appreciation for their presence in the natural world.

Science-Inspired Tree Photography

The growing interest in scientific themes is influencing tree photography. This trend involves capturing images that reflect scientific concepts, such as the biology of trees or their role in ecosystems.

Science-inspired tree photography not only captures the aesthetic beauty of trees but also educates viewers about their ecological importance and scientific aspects.

The latest trends in tree photography reflect a diverse and creative approach to capturing the essence of trees. From computational and 3D photography to cinematic and science-inspired images, these trends showcase the beauty, complexity, and significance of trees in our environment.

As photography continues to evolve, it will undoubtedly keep playing a crucial role in highlighting the importance of trees and forests, inspiring both appreciation and conservation efforts.

TREES IN FILM AND MEDIA - SYMBOLISM AND REPRESENTATION

Symbolism in Cinema

Symbolism in film uses visual cues to represent more significant concepts or ideas, allowing filmmakers to communicate complex themes subtly and artfully. Trees in cinema often serve as symbols, embodying themes of life, growth, or nature's cycles.

The Role of Trees in Character Symbolism

Character symbolism can include trees to represent a character's traits or growth. For instance, in "Forrest Gump," the feather symbolizes Forrest's life journey and philosophy, similar to a tree being carried through life by circumstances beyond its control yet growing and adapting optimistically.

Religious and Spiritual Symbolism of Trees

Religious symbolism in film often employs trees to represent spiritual concepts. In "The Matrix," the protagonist, Neo, is a symbol of religious saviors or messiahs, akin to the biblical

Tree of Life, representing knowledge, eternal life, and the interconnectivity of all living things.

Nature Symbolism with Trees

Nature symbolism in cinema uses trees to represent deeper meanings, ideas, or emotions. For example, rain symbolizing freedom in "The Shawshank Redemption" can be mirrored in scenes where trees are shown in torrential rain, symbolizing rebirth or cleansing.

Animal Symbolism and Trees

Animal symbolism in films can intertwine with trees, representing various themes. For instance, a bird resting on a tree branch might symbolize freedom or perspective.

Object Symbolism Involving Trees

Object symbolism in films often includes trees or parts of trees (like leaves or branches) to convey complex ideas and emotions, making the stories more captivating and meaningful.

Famous Trees in Films

- In "Harry Potter," the Whomping Willow symbolizes protection and hidden secrets.
- Treebeard from "The Lord of the Rings" embodies wisdom, strength, and the guardianship of nature.
- The Tree of Life in "The Lion King" represents knowledge and the cycle of life.

- Grandmother Willow in "Pocahontas" is a symbol of guidance, wisdom, and spiritual connection.
- The apple trees in "The Wizard of Oz" represent temptation and the unexpected challenges in life.

Trees and Metaphors in Film

Trees often serve as metaphors in films, drawing comparisons between their growth, resilience, and the human condition. They can symbolize endurance, stability, or change, reflecting the narrative's themes or characters' journeys.

Trees in film and media are powerful symbols, representing a wide range of themes from growth and life to wisdom and spirituality. Their presence enriches narratives, providing depth and a richer understanding of the artistic vision.

Specific Use of Trees in Various Film Genres

In dramas, trees often symbolize emotional states or social commentaries, such as resilience in the face of adversity or the interplay between humans and nature.

In science fiction and fantasy, trees can represent mythical elements or futuristic concepts, acting as portals to other worlds or as sentient beings with profound wisdom.

Cultural Significance of Trees in Cinema

Trees in films often carry cultural significance, reflecting the beliefs and values of different societies. For example, in many Asian films, trees are depicted as sacred and are central to the narrative, symbolizing life, death, and rebirth.

In Western cinema, trees are frequently used to depict the passage of time, transitions in life, or as settings for pivotal moments in the storyline.

Contemporary Filmmakers' Use of Trees as Symbols

Modern filmmakers are increasingly using trees to address environmental concerns, such as deforestation or climate change, using them as symbols of the planet's fragility and the need for conservation.

Trees are also used to explore themes of connectivity and communication, reflecting the interconnectedness of all life forms and the impact of human actions on nature.

Trees as a Reflection of Characters' Inner Worlds

In psychological dramas or character studies, trees often mirror the internal struggles or growth of characters, serving as metaphors for their emotional journeys or transformations.

The presence or absence of trees in certain scenes can also subtly indicate a character's isolation, growth, or connection to their environment.

Techniques in Depicting Trees in Film

Cinematography plays a crucial role in how trees are depicted in films. The use of lighting, angles, and framing can emphasize the symbolic importance of trees in the narrative.

Special effects, such as CGI, are often used to bring mythical or extraordinary trees to life, enhancing their impact and significance within the story.

Trees in film and media serve as powerful symbols and narrative devices, reflecting a wide array of themes and emotions. From representing cultural beliefs to highlighting environmental issues, trees continue to be a significant element in cinematic storytelling, enriching the viewers' experience and understanding of the film's deeper messages.

TOWARD THE FUTURE

INNOVATIVE USES OF TREES - TECHNOLOGY AND BEYOND

Technology Integration in Tree Care

Advances in technology are revolutionizing tree care. Drones now conduct aerial inspections, providing detailed imagery and data analysis for accurate health assessments. GPS technology enhances the mapping and monitoring of tree populations, ensuring more precise and efficient care.

Eco-Friendly and Organic Practices

The shift towards eco-friendly and organic practices in arboriculture is evident. The use of biodegradable products for tree treatments and holistic approaches to pest and disease management minimizes chemical use and promotes biodiversity.

Urban Forestry Advancements

Innovative strategies integrate trees into urban planning, considering species best suited for city environments and pollution tolerance. This approach aims to develop tree-friendly infrastructure that supports urban green spaces.

Climate-Adaptive Arboriculture

Arboriculture is increasingly focusing on climate-adaptive practices. This includes selecting tree species that can withstand changing climate conditions and managing resources to mitigate the effects of extreme weather events.

Enhanced Training and Safety Measures

The industry has improved safety protocols and equipment to protect arborists and property. Public education initiatives raise awareness about proper tree care and the role of arborists in maintaining tree health.

Artificial Trees for Renewable Energy

Research in renewable energy has explored the concept of artificial trees. These trees use piezoelectrics, a method where certain materials can generate electricity when bent or squeezed. However, harnessing this energy efficiently remains a challenge.

LIDAR in Forest Management

LIDAR, a remote sensing method, is used to map forest canopy surfaces, tree structures, and underlying topography. This technology helps in understanding biodiversity needs and managing forests more effectively.

DNA Testing for Biodiversity

DNA testing is employed to chart biodiversity within forest ecosystems. This technique helps in making informed decisions for the health of the forest, especially in areas rich in biodiversity.

Drones in Forest Maintenance

Drones, or unmanned aerial surveillance systems, are increasingly used in forest maintenance. They provide critical data for wildland fire response and other natural resource applications, enhancing the safety and efficiency of forest management.

Digital Thinning Prescriptions

The forestry sector utilizes digital tools for vegetation management, including electronic prescriptions for thinnings. This innovation enables more efficient and precise management of forest thinning processes.

Satellite Monitoring for Reforestation

Satellites equipped with high-resolution cameras and sensors help monitor the success or failure of reforestation projects. This large-scale data collection is vital for understanding how trees are faring and making adjustments to reforestation efforts.

Tree Sensors for Detailed Monitoring

Advanced sensors attached to trees enable real-time, detailed observation of forest growth and health. These sensors provide crucial data for long-term monitoring of reforested areas.

The intersection of technology and tree care is leading to innovative practices that enhance the health of trees and the environment. From drones and LIDAR to DNA testing and artificial trees, these advancements are reshaping the future of arboriculture and forest management.

Role of Technology in Tree Conservation

Technology plays a crucial role in tree conservation, especially in monitoring and managing protected forest areas. Automated sensors and satellite imagery provide valuable data on forest conditions, helping to protect against illegal logging and forest fires.

AI and Machine Learning in Forestry

Artificial intelligence (AI) and machine learning are being utilized to analyze large datasets in forestry. This technology aids in predicting forest growth, identifying disease outbreaks, and optimizing tree planting strategies.

AI-driven models can simulate various scenarios to determine the best approaches for forest conservation and sustainable management.

Trees and Climate Change Combat

Advanced technologies are being employed to evaluate the role of trees in combating climate change. This includes assessing their carbon sequestration capabilities and understanding their impact on local climates.

AI algorithms are used to identify areas most suitable for reforestation and to monitor the health of trees in these newly forested areas.

Technology in Urban Tree Management

In urban areas, technology aids in the management and maintenance of trees. Mobile apps and GPS mapping enable city planners and residents to track the health and growth of urban trees.

Sensors attached to trees monitor environmental conditions, providing data that informs urban planning decisions to optimize the benefits of urban greenery.

Futuristic Tree Technologies

Innovations in biotechnology are exploring the creation of genetically modified trees with enhanced growth rates or resistance to diseases and pests.

Research into bioenergy and biomaterials is developing new ways to use trees for sustainable energy production and environmentally friendly products.

Educational Programs and Public Engagement

Technology also plays a role in educational programs about tree conservation. Interactive apps and virtual reality experiences are used to engage the public and raise awareness about the importance of trees.

Online platforms facilitate community involvement in tree planting and conservation projects, promoting a collective effort towards a greener future.

The integration of cutting-edge technology in tree care and forest management is ushering in a new era of sustainable and efficient practices. From AI and machine learning to drones and satellite monitoring, these innovations are vital in ensuring the health of trees and forests, combating climate change, and fostering a deeper connection between communities and their natural environments.

TREES IN URBAN PLANNING - GREEN CITIES

The Role of Trees in Urban Environments

In the context of urban planning, trees play an indispensable role in creating sustainable, healthy, and aesthetically pleasing cities. They act as natural air purifiers, removing pollutants and providing cleaner air. Trees also mitigate urban heat islands through shade and evapotranspiration, significantly reducing temperatures in built-up areas. Additionally, urban trees contribute to biodiversity, offering habitats for various species within city limits.

Strategic Planting and Maintenance

The strategic placement of trees is critical for maximizing their benefits. For example, planting deciduous trees on the south and west sides of buildings can provide shade during summer and allow sunlight in winter. The choice of species is also crucial to ensure resilience against pests, diseases, and varying urban conditions. Regular maintenance, including pruning and health assessments, ensures trees remain safe and healthy in urban settings.

Urban Trees and Mental Health

Urban trees have a profound impact on mental health. Green spaces with trees provide residents with places for relaxation and recreation, reducing stress and promoting psychological well-being. The presence of trees in urban areas has been linked to reduced rates of anxiety, depression, and other mental health issues.

Stormwater Management and Erosion Control

Trees play a vital role in stormwater management. Their roots absorb and filter water, reducing runoff and preventing erosion. This natural water management system is essential in cities where impermeable surfaces are prevalent, helping to mitigate flooding risks and protect water quality in urban watersheds.

Economic Benefits

Urban trees offer significant economic benefits. They increase property values and attract businesses and tourists. Trees also reduce energy costs by providing shade in summer and windbreaks in winter. Additionally, green spaces can foster community engagement and social cohesion, contributing to more vibrant and desirable urban environments.

Challenges and Solutions

Urban environments pose specific challenges for trees, including limited soil space, pollution, and physical damage. Innovative solutions like structured soil systems and green roofs are being employed to overcome these challenges. The use of technology in monitoring tree health and growth patterns is also on the rise, aiding in better management and planning.

Community Involvement and Education

Community involvement is key in urban tree initiatives.

Educating residents about the benefits of urban trees fosters a sense of ownership and responsibility. Community-led planting and maintenance programs can strengthen the bond between citizens and their urban environment.

Integrating Trees in Urban Design

Modern urban design increasingly incorporates trees as essential elements. From street trees to public parks and green belts, integrating greenery into city planning is vital for sustainable urban development. Architects and planners are recognizing the need for green spaces in urban design, not only for environmental reasons but also for enhancing quality of life.

Impact on Wildlife

Urban trees provide critical habitats for wildlife in cities, creating a connection between urban areas and nature. They support birds, insects, and small mammals, contributing to urban biodiversity and offering residents opportunities to experience nature in their immediate surroundings.

The Future of Urban Trees

Looking towards the future, the role of trees in urban environments is set to expand. With the increasing emphasis on sustainable development and climate change mitigation, urban trees are more important than ever. Cities around the world are setting ambitious targets for planting and maintaining trees, recognizing their value in creating healthier, more resilient urban landscapes.

THE LEGACY WE LEAVE - TREES AND FUTURE GENERATIONS

Ensuring a Sustainable Future through Tree Preservation

Trees are fundamental to the health of our planet and the well-being of future generations. They play a vital role in maintaining environmental balance, providing oxygen, sequestering carbon, and offering habitats for countless species. In the face of increasing deforestation and climate change, it is crucial to preserve and protect trees to ensure a sustainable future.

The Multifaceted Benefits of Trees

Trees offer a multitude of environmental, social, and economic benefits. They improve air quality by absorbing pollutants, mitigate climate change through carbon sequestration, and provide essential habitats for wildlife. Socially, trees contribute to mental and physical well-being, offering spaces for recreation and relaxation. Economically, they provide resources like lumber, boost tourism, and increase property values. Preserving trees is not just about environmental stewardship; it's about ensuring the quality of life for future generations.

The Role of Reforestation and Forest Management

Reforestation and sustainable forest management are key to preserving trees. Planting new trees and protecting existing forests can restore damaged ecosystems, improve biodiversity, and strengthen resilience against climate change. Careful management ensures that forests continue to provide their crucial ecological services while also meeting human needs.

The Importance of Local and Global Initiatives

Local and global initiatives play a critical role in tree preservation. Community-driven tree planting and maintenance programs foster a sense of stewardship and connect people to their environment. On a larger scale, international efforts to combat deforestation and promote sustainable forestry practices are essential for preserving the world's forest heritage.

Trees in Urban Environments

Urban trees are especially important for future generations. They provide natural cooling, reduce pollution, and enhance the livability of cities. Integrating trees into urban planning is vital for creating sustainable and resilient urban spaces.

Education and Awareness

Educating the public about the importance of trees is crucial for their preservation. Awareness campaigns and educational programs can inspire action and encourage responsible practices. Teaching children about the significance of trees instills a sense of responsibility towards the environment from an early age.

Challenges and Solutions

Preserving trees faces several challenges, including urbanization, industrial agriculture, and climate change. Addressing these requires innovative solutions like urban forestry, agroforestry, and the use of technology in monitoring and managing forest resources.

The Legacy of Trees

The legacy we leave with trees is a testament to our commitment to the environment and future generations. By preserving trees, we ensure a healthier, more sustainable world. This legacy is not just about the trees themselves, but about the message of stewardship, respect, and responsibility we pass on.

A Call to Action

The preservation of trees is a collective responsibility that requires action from individuals, communities, governments, and international organizations. Planting a tree is more than an environmental act; it is a commitment to future generations, a statement of hope and care for the planet.

The Future of Our Forests

The future of our forests lies in our hands. By protecting and preserving trees today, we secure the environmental, social, and economic benefits they provide for future generations. This is our opportunity to leave a lasting, green legacy.

APPENDIX A: GLOSSARY OF TERMS

Arboriculture: The science and practice of tree care and management, often focused on individual trees in urban or landscaped settings.

Biodiversity: The variety of life in a particular habitat or ecosystem, including the range of plant and animal species.

Cambium: A thin layer of tissue between the bark and wood in a tree, responsible for the growth of new bark and wood cells.

Carbon Sequestration: The process of capturing and storing atmospheric carbon dioxide. Trees perform this naturally through photosynthesis.

Deciduous: Referring to trees that shed their leaves annually, typically in the autumn.

Dendrochronology: The scientific method of dating based on the analysis of patterns of tree rings, also known as tree-ring dating.

Ecosystem Services: Benefits provided by ecosystems to humans, including clean air and water, pollination of crops, and carbon storage.

Mycorrhizal Fungi: A type of fungus that forms a symbiotic relationship with the roots of a tree, enhancing nutrient and water absorption.

Phloem: The vascular tissue in plants that conducts sugars and other metabolic products downward from the leaves.

Photosynthesis: The process by which green plants and some other organisms use sunlight to synthesize nutrients from carbon dioxide and water.

Respiration: The process in which trees and other living organisms convert nutrients and oxygen into energy, releasing carbon dioxide as a byproduct.

Savannah: A grassy plain in tropical and subtropical regions, with few trees.

Transpiration: The process of water movement through a plant and its evaporation from aerial parts like leaves, stems, and flowers.

Xylem: The vascular tissue in plants that conducts water and dissolved nutrients upward from the root and also helps to form the woody element in the stem.

APPENDIX B: RESOURCES FOR FURTHER READING

This appendix offers a curated list of additional resources for readers interested in exploring the themes of "Whispers of the Green: Unveiling the Mystical Language of Trees" in greater depth. These resources include books, documentaries, and online platforms that provide extensive information on various aspects of trees and forests.

Books

1. **"The Hidden Life of Trees" by Peter Wohlleben**: An exploration of the social networks and complex lives of trees.

2. **"The Overstory" by Richard Powers**: A novel intertwining the lives of its characters with the lives of trees, highlighting the connection between humans and nature.

3. **"Braiding Sweetgrass" by Robin Wall Kimmerer**: A blend of indigenous wisdom and scientific knowledge about plants and their significance in our lives.

4. **"Forest Bathing" by Dr. Qing Li**: An introduction to the Japanese practice of Shinrin-Yoku, exploring its

scientifically-proven benefits.

5. **"Ancient Trees: Portraits of Time" by Beth Moon**: A photographic journey to some of the world's most ancient trees.

Documentaries and Films

1. **"Intelligent Trees"**: Featuring Peter Wohlleben and Suzanne Simard, this documentary delves into the communication and social networks of trees.

2. **"Call of the Forest: The Forgotten Wisdom of Trees"**: A film exploring the role of trees in environmental health and personal well-being.

3. **"The Man Who Planted Trees"**: An animated short film about a shepherd's long and successful single-handed effort to re-forest a desolate valley.

Online Resources

1. **Tree Identification Guides**: Online tools and apps for identifying tree species.

2. Global Forest Watch: An interactive online platform providing data and tools for monitoring forests.

3. **Ancient Tree Inventory**: A living database of ancient trees, compiled by the Woodland Trust.

4. **TED Talks on Trees and Forests**: A collection of insightful TED Talks covering various aspects of trees and forests.

5. i-Tree: A suite of tools for assessing and managing forests and community trees.

APPENDIX C: LINKS TO ACADEMIC PAPERS AND JOURNALS

This appendix provides a selection of academic papers and journals that delve deeper into the scientific research and studies referenced in "Whispers of the Green: Unveiling the Mystical Language of Trees." These resources offer in-depth insights into various aspects of tree biology, forest ecology, and environmental science.

Academic Papers

1. **"The Worldwide Leaf Economics Spectrum" by Wright et al.**
    - **Topic**: Examines the global variations in leaf traits across plant species.
    - **Journal**: Nature
    - **Available from**: Nature.com
2. **"Mycorrhizal Association as a Primary Control of the CO2 Fertilization Effect" by Terrer et al.**
    - **Topic**: Studies the impact of mycorrhizal fungi on plant responses to CO2 increases.
    - **Journal**: Science

- **Available from**: ScienceMag.org

3. **"Tree Rings and Climate: Sharpening the Focus" by Hughes et al.**
    - **Topic**: Discusses the use of dendrochronology in understanding climate changes.
    - **Journal**: Journal of Geophysical Research
    - **Available from**: AGU Journals

4. **"Forest Biodiversity, Ecosystem Functioning and the Provision of Ecosystem Services" by Gamfeldt et al.**
    - **Topic**: Explores the relationship between forest biodiversity and ecosystem services.
    - **Journal**: Biodiversity and Conservation
    - **Available from**: Springer.com

5. **"Global Forest Carbon Uptake: The Role of Forest Biomass Density Changes" by Liu et al.**
    - **Topic**: Analyzes the role of forest biomass in global carbon uptake.
    - **Journal**: Scientific Reports
    - **Available from**: Nature.com

Journals

1. **Journal of Forestry**
    - **Description**: Covers a wide range of topics including forest management, ecology, and conservation.
    - **Available from**: Oxford Academic

2. **Forest Ecology and Management**

- **Description**: Focuses on the management, conservation, and sustainable development of forest ecosystems.
- **Available from**: Elsevier

3. **Tree Physiology**
    - **Description**: Publishes research on the physiology of trees, tree functioning, and responses to environmental pressures.
    - **Available from**: Oxford Academic

4. **Canadian Journal of Forest Research**
    - **Description**: Offers articles on forest research, including forest management and pathogen resistance.
    - **Available from**: NRC Research Press

5. **Global Change Biology**
    - **Description**: Explores the effects of global changes, including climate change, on biological systems, especially forests.
    - **Available from**: Wiley Online Library

APPENDIX D: TREE IDENTIFICATION GUIDE

This appendix serves as a practical guide for readers interested in identifying various tree species mentioned in "Whispers of the Green: Unveiling the Mystical Language of Trees." The guide provides descriptions, key characteristics, and visual aids to help differentiate between species, focusing on those common to different climates and geographical regions.

Common Tree Species

Oak (Quercus spp.)

- **Characteristics**: Robust size, lobed leaves, and distinctive acorns.
- **Bark**: Rough, with deep ridges.
- **Leaves**: Vary by species, generally lobed with rounded or pointed tips.
- **Habitat**: Predominant in temperate forests of the Northern Hemisphere.

Maple (Acer spp.)

- **Characteristics**: Known for vibrant fall color and "helicopter" seed pods.

- **Bark**: Smooth in young trees, becoming rough and cracked with age.
- **Leaves**: Typically palmate with 3-9 lobes, varying widely among species.
- **Habitat**: Common in North America, Europe, and Asia.

Pine (Pinus spp.)

- **Characteristics**: Evergreen conifers with needle-like leaves.
- **Bark**: Thick and scaly, varies among species.
- **Leaves**: Needles, often in bundles of 2-5.
- **Habitat**: Diverse environments, from Arctic Circle to tropical regions.

Willow (Salix spp.)

- **Characteristics**: Graceful, drooping branches, and slender leaves.
- **Bark**: Smooth on younger trees, becoming deeply fissured with age.
- **Leaves**: Long, narrow, and typically finely serrated.
- **Habitat**: Prefers moist soils near water bodies.

Birch (Betula spp.)

- **Characteristics**: Notable for peeling bark and slender form.
- **Bark**: Smooth and often white or silver, peeling in horizontal strips.
- **Leaves**: Triangular or ovate with serrated edges.

- **Habitat**: Northern temperate and boreal climates.

Redwood (Sequoia and Sequoiadendron spp.)

- **Characteristics**: Among the tallest trees, with a thick, fibrous bark.
- **Bark**: Reddish-brown, deeply furrowed, and spongy.
- **Leaves**: Needle-like in young trees, becoming scale-like in maturity.
- **Habitat**: Coastal regions of northern California.

Banyan (Ficus benghalensis)

- **Characteristics**: Large, spreading tree with aerial prop roots.
- **Bark**: Gray and smooth.
- **Leaves**: Large, leathery, and oval-shaped with a pointed tip.
- **Habitat**: Native to India and Pakistan, often found in tropical climates.

Magnolia (Magnolia spp.)

- **Characteristics**: Known for large, fragrant flowers and glossy leaves.
- **Bark**: Smooth, gray, and relatively thin.
- **Leaves**: Large, glossy, and often leathery, ranging from ovate to elliptical.
- **Habitat**: Predominantly found in East Asia and the Americas, thriving in temperate and tropical climates.

Beech (Fagus spp.)

- **Characteristics**: Smooth gray bark and elliptical leaves with wavy edges.
- **Bark**: Smooth and light gray, often resembling elephant skin.
- **Leaves**: Simple, alternate, with a pointed tip and wavy margin.
- **Habitat**: Widely found in Europe, Asia, and North America in temperate zones.

Cedar (Cedrus spp.)

- **Characteristics**: Coniferous evergreen with needle-like leaves and woody cones.
- **Bark**: Thick, fibrous, and deeply fissured, often with a reddish hue.
- **Leaves**: Needle-like, clustered in whorls on short shoots.
- **Habitat**: Native to the mountains of the western Himalayas and the Mediterranean.

Eucalyptus (Eucalyptus spp.)

- **Characteristics**: Fast-growing trees known for their oil and peeling bark.
- **Bark**: Varies among species, often peeling in strips to reveal different colors.
- **Leaves**: Long, narrow, and aromatic, often hanging downwards.
- **Habitat**: Indigenous to Australia, but widely cultivated in other parts of the world.

Cherry (Prunus spp.)

- **Characteristics**: Known for their spring blossom and fruit.
- **Bark**: Smooth with horizontal bands, can become rough in older trees.
- **Leaves**: Simple, alternate, with a serrated margin.
- **Habitat**: Widespread in the Northern Hemisphere, particularly in temperate regions.

Aspen (Populus tremula)

- **Characteristics**: Notable for their trembling leaves and smooth, white bark.
- **Bark**: Smooth and pale, often with black knots or scars.
- **Leaves**: Rounded with fine teeth on the margins, fluttering in the breeze.
- **Habitat**: Widely distributed across cooler regions of the Northern Hemisphere.

Baobab (Adansonia spp.)

- **Characteristics**: Known for their massive trunks and long lifespan.
- **Bark**: Thick, fibrous, and fire-resistant.
- **Leaves**: Hand-shaped, divided into five to seven finger-like leaflets.
- **Habitat**: Native to Madagascar, mainland Africa, and Australia, thriving in arid regions.

Ginkgo (Ginkgo biloba)

- **Characteristics**: Unique fan-shaped leaves and known as a living fossil.

- **Bark**: Rough, often deeply furrowed, grayish-brown.
- **Leaves**: Fan-shaped, sometimes bilobed, turning bright yellow in autumn.
- **Habitat**: Originally from China, now widely planted worldwide.

Hawthorn (Crataegus spp.)

- **Characteristics**: Small, often thorny trees known for their white or pink blossoms and red berries.
- **Bark**: Gray to reddish-brown, typically rough and scaly.
- **Leaves**: Variable shapes, generally lobed and toothed.
- **Habitat**: Commonly found in temperate regions of North America, Europe, and Asia.

Sequoia (Sequoiadendron giganteum)

- **Characteristics**: Among the largest trees in the world, known for their immense height and girth.
- **Bark**: Thick, fibrous, deeply furrowed, and reddish-brown.
- **Leaves**: Small, scale-like, and overlapping, forming a dense covering.
- **Habitat**: Native to the western slopes of the Sierra Nevada mountains in California.

Sycamore (Platanus spp.)

- **Characteristics**: Large, fast-growing trees known for their mottled exfoliating bark.

- **Bark**: Mottled with patches of white, tan, and green, peeling off in flakes.
- **Leaves**: Large, palmate, with three to five lobes.
- **Habitat**: Found in temperate regions, often near rivers and in urban landscapes.

Ash (Fraxinus spp.)

- **Characteristics**: Known for their compound leaves and strong, elastic wood.
- **Bark**: Gray to brown, with a distinct pattern of diamond-shaped ridges.
- **Leaves**: Opposite, pinnately compound with several leaflets.
- **Habitat**: Widespread in Europe, Asia, and North America, particularly in cool climates.

Linden (Tilia spp.)

- **Characteristics**: Valued for fragrant flowers and heart-shaped leaves.
- **Bark**: Gray to brown, becoming furrowed with age.
- **Leaves**: Simple, heart-shaped, with serrated margins.
- **Habitat**: Common in the temperate Northern Hemisphere.

Alder (Alnus spp.)

- **Characteristics**: Known for their catkins and ability to improve soil fertility.
- **Bark**: Smooth and gray in young trees; older trees have darker, cracked bark.

- **Leaves**: Simple, rounded or oval, often with a serrated margin.
- **Habitat**: Commonly found near streams, rivers, and wetlands in temperate climates.

Fir (Abies spp.)

- **Characteristics**: Evergreen conifers known for their symmetrical shape and unique cone structure.
- **Bark**: Generally smooth and gray when young, becoming furrowed with age.
- **Leaves**: Needle-like, generally attached individually to the branches.
- **Habitat**: Predominantly found in mountainous regions of Europe, Asia, and North America.

Hemlock (Tsuga spp.)

- **Characteristics**: Evergreen conifers with a graceful, drooping form.
- **Bark**: Rough and scaly, often dark brown.
- **Leaves**: Small, needle-like, arranged in a feathery pattern.
- **Habitat**: Mostly found in cool, moist areas of North America and Asia.

Palm (Arecaceae family)

- **Characteristics**: Known for their unbranched trunks and large, fan-shaped leaves.
- **Bark**: Varies among species; generally smooth with scars from fallen leaves.
- **Leaves**: Large, either fan-shaped (palmate) or

feather-shaped (pinnate).

- **Habitat**: Predominantly found in tropical and subtropical regions.

Dogwood (Cornus spp.)

- **Characteristics**: Known for their beautiful spring blossoms and distinctive bark.
- **Bark**: Patterned with a mosaic of small, square blocks in mature trees.
- **Leaves**: Simple, opposite, with an oval to lanceolate shape.
- **Habitat**: Widely distributed in temperate regions of the Northern Hemisphere.

Elm (Ulmus spp.)

- **Characteristics**: Notable for their distinctive leaf shape and vase-like growth form.
- **Bark**: Dark, deeply furrowed, and often cross-grained.
- **Leaves**: Simple, asymmetrical at the base, with serrated edges.
- **Habitat**: Common in temperate regions, often used in urban landscaping.

Cypress (Cupressus spp.)

- **Characteristics**: Evergreen conifers with a distinctive conical shape.
- **Bark**: Fibrous, peeling in strips, often gray to reddish-brown.
- **Leaves**: Scale-like, closely appressed to the branches.

- **Habitat**: Native to various regions, including the Mediterranean and North America.

Poplar (Populus spp.)

- **Characteristics**: Tall, fast-growing trees, often with a columnar shape.
- **Bark**: Rough and furrowed in older trees; younger trees have smoother bark.
- **Leaves**: Generally triangular or diamond-shaped, with a flattened stem that makes leaves tremble in the wind.
- **Habitat**: Common in temperate regions of the Northern Hemisphere, often near water sources.

Kauri (Agathis australis)

- **Characteristics**: Massive evergreen trees, known for their longevity and large trunks.
- **Bark**: Smooth, gray, and peeling in flakes or strips.
- **Leaves**: Leathery, broad, and oval-shaped, often arranged in a spiral pattern.
- **Habitat**: Native to the northern part of New Zealand's North Island.

Spruce (Picea spp.)

- **Characteristics**: Evergreen conifers with a pyramidal shape and hanging cones.
- **Bark**: Thin and scaly, often flaking off in small, circular plates.
- **Leaves**: Needle-like, attached individually to the branches, often with a sharp point.

- **Habitat**: Predominantly found in boreal regions and the northern temperate zone.

Monkey Puzzle (Araucaria araucana)

- **Characteristics**: An ancient conifer with a unique appearance, featuring stiff, overlapping leaves.
- **Bark**: Thick and scaly, gray to brown in color.
- **Leaves**: Broad, sharp, and scale-like, covering the branches densely.
- **Habitat**: Native to central and southern Chile and western Argentina.

Tulip Tree (Liriodendron tulipifera)

- **Characteristics**: Known for its distinct tulip-shaped flowers and leaves.
- **Bark**: Grayish-brown, with deep furrows and flat-topped ridges.
- **Leaves**: Unique shape, resembling a tulip, with four lobes.
- **Habitat**: Common in the eastern United States, found in mixed hardwood forests.

Mango Tree (Mangifera indica)

- **Characteristics**: Evergreen trees known for their succulent fruit and dense crown.
- **Bark**: Dark brown to black, rough and fissured.
- **Leaves**: Simple, lanceolate, and leathery, with a shiny surface.
- **Habitat**: Indigenous to South Asia, extensively cultivated in tropical regions.

Teak (Tectona grandis)

- **Characteristics**: Large deciduous trees valued for their durable hardwood.
- **Bark**: Gray to brown, deeply fissured in older trees.
- **Leaves**: Large, opposite, ovate, and hairy beneath.
- **Habitat**: Native to India, Myanmar, and Indonesia, cultivated in other tropical regions.

Identifying Features

- **Leaf Shape and Arrangement**: One of the primary ways to identify a tree species is by observing the shape, size, and arrangement of its leaves.
- **Bark Texture and Color**: Bark characteristics can be distinctive, varying greatly between species.
- **Fruit and Seeds**: The type of fruit or seeds produced by a tree can be a key identifying feature.
- **Overall Tree Shape and Size**: The general shape and size of a tree, including its branching pattern, can provide clues to its identity.
- **Seasonal Changes**: Consider how a tree changes with seasons, including leaf color in autumn and flowering patterns.
- **Habitat and Location**: Some trees are specific to certain environments or geographic regions.
- **Use of Technology**: Utilize tree identification apps and online databases for assistance.

- **Bud Characteristics**: The shape, size, and arrangement of buds can be a helpful identification tool, especially in winter.

- **Tree Silhouette**: The overall shape or silhouette of a tree can be distinctive and is often used in species identification.

- **Cone or Seed Structure**: In conifers, the size, shape, and arrangement of cones are key identifying features.

- **Wood Characteristics**: The color, grain, and texture of the wood are often used to identify tree species, particularly in forestry and woodworking.

- **Growth Habit**: The natural growth pattern of a tree, whether upright, spreading, or weeping, can assist in identification.

APPENDIX E: CONSERVATION ORGANIZATIONS AND INITIATIVES

This appendix lists various organizations and initiatives dedicated to tree conservation, reforestation, and forest protection. These groups work at local, national, and global levels and offer opportunities for involvement and support in preserving and enhancing tree populations.

Global Organizations

1. **Arbor Day Foundation**
    - **Mission**: Inspire people to plant, nurture, and celebrate trees.
    - **Activities**: Tree planting, educational programs, community tree recovery.
    - **Website**: arborday.org

2. **Trees for the Future**
    - **Mission**: Improve the livelihoods of impoverished farmers by revitalizing degraded lands.
    - **Activities**: Agroforestry, sustainable

farming practices, tree planting.
- **Website**: trees.org

3. **Rainforest Alliance**
    - **Mission**: Build strong forests and healthy communities through sustainable practices.
    - **Activities**: Certification programs, climate-smart agriculture, forest conservation.
    - **Website**: rainforest-alliance.org

4. **World Wildlife Fund (WWF) - Forests for Life Programme**
    - **Mission**: Conserve the world's most important forests to sustain nature's diversity.
    - **Activities**: Protecting forest lands, combating illegal logging, promoting sustainable forestry.
    - **Website**: worldwildlife.org

National and Regional Organizations

5. **The Woodland Trust (UK)**
    - **Mission**: Protect and restore ancient woodlands and encourage new planting.
    - **Activities**: Woodland restoration, wildlife protection, public engagement.
    - **Website**: woodlandtrust.org.uk

6. **American Forests**
    - **Mission**: Create healthy and resilient forests from cities to wilderness.

- **Activities**: Urban forest expansion, wildland restoration, public policy advocacy.
- **Website**: americanforests.org

7. **Tree Canada**
    - **Mission**: Promote the planting and nurturing of trees in Canada.
    - **Activities**: Urban greening, reforestation, community engagement.
    - **Website**: treecanada.ca

Community and Grassroots Initiatives

8. **Local Tree Planting Organizations**
    - Many communities have local tree planting organizations or initiatives. These groups often work on urban tree planting, local reforestation, and educational outreach.

9. **School and University Programs**
    - Educational institutions often have programs or clubs dedicated to environmental stewardship, including tree planting and conservation efforts.

10. **Community Forest Management Groups**
    - In many regions, community-led initiatives manage and protect local forests, focusing on sustainable practices and local ecosystem health.

Volunteer and Citizen Science Opportunities

- Many conservation organizations offer volunteer

opportunities, allowing individuals to participate in tree planting and forest conservation activities.

- Citizen science projects, often organized by universities or research institutions, invite public participation in data collection and environmental monitoring.

These organizations and initiatives provide avenues for individuals to contribute to tree conservation efforts, either through direct action, donations, or advocacy. Their work is vital in maintaining healthy forest ecosystems and combating global environmental challenges.

APPENDIX F: INTERACTIVE ONLINE RESOURCES

This appendix lists a variety of interactive online resources that offer educational and engaging experiences related to trees and forestry. These resources range from virtual tree identification tools to interactive maps and databases, providing valuable information for enthusiasts, students, and professionals alike.

Tree Identification Tools and Apps

1. **Leafsnap**
   - **Description**: An electronic field guide developed by researchers from Columbia University, the University of Maryland, and the Smithsonian Institution, using visual recognition to help identify tree species from photographs of their leaves.
   - **Website/App**: leafsnap.com
2. **Virginia Tech Tree ID**
   - **Description**: An online guide created by Virginia Tech, offering a comprehensive database of trees with detailed information and imagery for identification.

- **Website**: dendro.cnre.vt.edu

3. **iNaturalist**
   - **Description**: A community-driven app and website for recording and sharing observations of biodiversity, including trees, with a feature for species identification and data sharing.
   - **Website/App**: inaturalist.org

Interactive Maps and Forest Data

4. **Global Forest Watch**
   - **Description**: Provides dynamic data and tools to monitor global forests and forest changes over time, useful for understanding deforestation and other environmental impacts.
   - **Website**: globalforestwatch.org

5. **Old-Growth Forest Network**
   - **Description**: An interactive map showcasing America's old-growth forests, aiming to connect citizens with ancient forests in their region.
   - **Website**: oldgrowthforest.net

6. **The National Tree Map**
   - **Description**: Maintained by the UK government, this map provides detailed information about the location and types of trees across the UK.
   - **Website**: gov.uk

Educational Platforms and Courses

7. **Coursera – Forests and Humans: From the Midwest to Madagascar**
    - **Description**: This course, offered by the University of Wisconsin-Madison, explores the complex interactions between forests and human beings across the globe.
    - **Website**: coursera.org

8. **TED-Ed Lessons on Trees**
    - **Description**: A collection of educational animated videos covering various topics about trees, their biology, and their importance to the environment.
    - **Website**: ed.ted.com

9. **Arbor Day Foundation – Tree Learning Center**
    - **Description**: Offers extensive resources on tree care, planting, and conservation, as well as educational materials for both adults and children.
    - **Website**: arborday.org

Citizen Science Projects

10. **The Tree Observation Project**
    - **Description**: A citizen science initiative that invites individuals to observe and record data on specific trees, contributing to a broader understanding of tree growth and health.
    - **Website**: treeobservation.org

11. **Project BudBurst**
    - **Description**: Focused on collecting data

on the timing of leafing, flowering, and fruiting phases of plants (phenology), helping scientists understand how plants respond to environmental changes.
- **Website**: budburst.org

These interactive online resources offer a wealth of information and participatory opportunities for those interested in expanding their knowledge and involvement in the world of trees and forestry.

THE END

Printed in Great Britain
by Amazon